TALKING WITH GOD

HENRY J. BARON

TALKING WITH GOD

Prayers, meditations &
conversations for God-seekers

EXXEL
PUBLISHING

323 Telegraph Rd. • Bellingham WA 98226-9901

Talking with God

© 2011 Henry J. Baron

Published in the United States by Exxel Publishing, 323 Telegraph Road, Bellingham, Washington 98226. Address all correspondence to:
Henry J. Baron, 2292 S. Thrush Ct. SE, Grand Rapids, MI 49546
Email: henrybaron@att.net
http://www.exxelpublishing.com

ISBN-13: 978-0-9703469-8-8
ISBN-10: 0-9703469-8-0

Printed in the United States of America

16 15 14 13 12 11   7 6 5 4 3 2 1

DEDICATIONS

*For Ruth, with gratitude for the constancy of her love,
encouragement, and support.
For my children and grandchildren who enrich my life.
For my Neland Church family who were my first readers and often
reminded me of the need for prayer and praise.*

CONTENTS

Acknowledgments

There was no original intent to have these talks with God circulate beyond the readers of the "Neland News," the monthly publication of my home church, Neland Avenue Christian Reformed Church. But fellow members would drop hints now and again that maybe I should consider gathering them in some kind of book form. None pressed the idea more than Dr. Anthony Hoekema, as we rode back and forth to council meetings together. Though he is no longer among us, I need to acknowledge, with gratitude, his urging and commendations that finally turned my reluctance into acquiescence.

Special thanks also to Judy Zylstra, former editor at Eerdmans Publishing, and daughter Cindy de Jong, former Coordinator of Worship at Calvin College, for their helpful advice when the book raced toward its final publishing stage.

And I will always be grateful for the encouragement, enthusiasm, and professional guidance of Dirk Wierenga, acquisitions editor, as well as for the good work of designers Dan van Loon and John Wollinka of Design Corps, and Ginny McFadden, copy editor.

INTRODUCTION

Christians pray.
Some pray much, like preachers and Christian school teachers.
Some pray occasionally, like at mealtime and bedtime.
Some pray seldom, publically or privately.

But all who genuinely pray believe or want to believe that God is,
    that God hears, that God cares.
And that takes a lot of faith in our time, in our world.
Such faith needs exercise and nurture.

Many Christians often wonder about God: what does God think
    about us —
about our culture, our politics, our priorities;
about poverty and prejudice among us;
about our church's controversies, policies, and practices.

We have many questions to ask, many problems to share, many
    perplexities to express.
And they need expression, or faith might falter,
suffocated by perturbations of the soul left unaddressed,
shriveled like a raisin in the sun, to use a poet's phrase.

Maybe we need to take our cue from Tevye in "Fiddler on the
    Roof" and make our talking with the God of our faith, hope,
    and love as natural as our discourse with family or friends.

These prayers and meditations were written over a 30-year
    period, roughly from 1978-2008, as a regular column in our
    congregation's monthly newspaper.
They sometimes reflect the events of the time and the concerns
    of my particular church family.
But events and concerns vary little according to time and
    location: wars, catastrophes, violence, and human tragedies

are part of our common experience, regardless of where and
   when we live.
In all times and in all places, we are called to practice and to live
   our faith.

Finally, these pieces are not meant to be read en masse.
Perhaps they serve their purpose best when read and pondered as
   devotional exercise, one at a sitting.
It is my prayer that these "Talks with God" will intensify the
   reader's desire to act justly, to love mercy, and to walk humbly
   with God.

WORSHIP

*For Christians, church is where our lives begin
and end.*

It's where we are baptized, married, and buried.

*It's the place of our worship and our spiritual
formation.*

*It's where we hear the Word and learn its
meaning.*

It's where our faith and understanding grow.

*It's where we are challenged to profess and live
our faith.*

*Sometimes we feel the Spirit's touch so tangibly
that our faith soars.*

*Sometimes we feel so hurt by disputes and tensions
that our faith flags.*

Sometimes questions turn into doubts.

But always the Lord of the Church keeps calling:

Come unto me...and learn of me.

Come, and worship.

BEFORE THE SERVICE

When we fill the pews on Sunday morning,
we come in varying states of strength and disrepair.
Sometimes we're so filled with grace and gratitude
that we want to pour out joy and praise.
Sometimes our minds are muddied with problems,
personal or professional, festering, unresolved.
Sometimes we're exhausted with the frustrations
or the pains and grieves of the week.
Sometimes our doubts clamor so loud
that we no longer hear your voice, oh God.

Yet, deep down, we come to worship with one basic need:
an encounter with the living Christ.
And though we will not see Jesus in the flesh,
we must see him with the inner eye of faith—
through stories and allusions and illustrations and images
that have inherent power to engage both heart and mind.
For if we fail to encounter Jesus on Sunday,
he will not likely be in our work and our relationships on
    Monday.

Lord, give us eyes to see
ears to hear
and faith to believe
when we encounter Jesus.
For that we pray as we bow our heads—
before the service.

❧ TO PONDER ❧
How do *you* prepare for worship?

Pastor as Shepherd

The Lord is my shepherd.
And our pastor is one too,
being about our Father's business.
He spends time among his sheep.
He listens to their voices, and they to his.
He understands what they say,
and intuits what they leave unsaid.
He has sensed their needs and shared their emotions.

He knows something of their challenges and frustrations,
of the tedium and the tensions,
of the loneliness and boredom,
of the fears and failures,
of the temptations and trials,
of the hopes and aspirations,
of the joys and sadness
that mark their daily lives.

But he also knows your Word, oh Lord.
He hears the Father's voice.
Among the sheep and among his books,
he listens, he reads, and searches for the meaning,
for the truth, and how it applies to daily life.

And then he makes a sermon.
A sermon for his sheep, shaped
by what he knows about his sheep
and what he understands about his Father's Word.
A sermon that derives its power from the sweat
and sweetness of having been about his Father's business.

Bless our pastor, Lord.

HOLY MOMENTS

If we have but eyes to see and sometimes ears to hear
we can't miss the glimpses that bring us close to you.

By the backyard trees now, the cardinal couple foraging,
then, hopping close to each other, the feathered beauties
take time out for a quick bird snuggle in the grass.

A pre-teen boy in a Sunday morning pew whispers in his
     father's ear,
the father smiles down into his son's eyes,
and the boy nestles closer to his dad.

In church school a four-year-old listens to her teacher
telling the Jesus story of the Good Samaritan.
When the teacher asks: why was the Samaritan good?
the child's eyes grow big and earnestly she says:
because he was like Jesus.
How was he like Jesus, Jennifer?
Because Jesus is like a shepherd,
he carries the sheep when it gets hurt.

A church family surprises a single Mom:
a ticket to fly back to her homeland far away,
to visit family and friends not seen for more than twenty years.
And suddenly, overwhelmed by so much love,
she cries and cries, till others too shed tears.

A minister preaches on God's forgiving grace,
when suddenly he pauses, like something's hit him.
When he looks up again, his eyes are brimming
and his voice is choking when he says:
"And someday, when even this pastor will find himself in heaven,
forgiven…"
then adds in a fierce whisper, tears now flowing down his face:

"why, that's the grace of God."
Parents by their bed late at night, on their knees,
praying, pleading for a wayward child…

An old couple in a nursing home, he nearly blind and she
    stone deaf.
She's reading to him now, about the mystery of what God
    has prepared
for those who love him, from I Cor. 2.
When she's done, he reaches for her hands, and prays;
the words not heard but felt, fall on her soul, then rise to
    heaven's ears.

Elders in a circle, intently listening to one's faith profession,
astonished, deeply moved by the testimony of one so young
who tells simply and profoundly of Jesus' claims on life.

Holy moments, for your holiness, oh God, is all around us,
if we have but eyes to see and ears to hear.

⮞ TO PONDER ⮜
What have been "holy moments" for *you?*

A Prayer for
a New Church Year

Fill thou my life, Lord…
Fill it with the excitement of new beginnings—at work, at
    school, at church.
Fill it with the steadiness of daily routine and the stimulation of
    surprise.
Fill it with confidence in the gifts I have from you,
that I may neither envy others nor grow discouraged with
    myself.
Fill it with balance that I may not be so consumed by job or
    family or church
as to render me ineffectual, or worse, hurtful to others.
Fill it with purpose that I may have a clear sense of what I'm
    living for
and why.
Fill it with goodness through the people and the things I love,
all that makes me glad to be alive,
to be a part of all that you have made.
Fill thou my life, O Lord my God
    in every part with praise.

Fill thou my life, Lord…
Fill it here at my own church.
Fill it with love and gratitude for the new pastor's family.
Fill it with the prayer that they may quickly adjust,
feel warmly embraced by us,
come to feel at home among us,
feel encouraged by our eagerness to grow in obedient
    discipleship.
Fill it with desire to do your work here:
preaching and teaching, leading and serving, planning
    and dreaming,
gathering and giving, worshipping and making music,

reaching out and touching lives that need food and work and
dignity and comfort.

Fill it with a holy passion to connect our lives to each other and
to God.

Fill thou my life, O Lord my God
…that my whole being may proclaim
thy being and thy ways.

Fill thou my life, Lord…

Fill it in this sadly broken but beautiful world.

Fill it with compassion for the suffering.

Fill it with your anger for all that's unjust, inhuman, evil.

Fill it with the will to make a holy difference in this world,

even if it's only in my own home, in my own church, and in the
voting booth.

Fill it with great joy at all that shines or even glimmers

with the glory and the grace of God—

in his creation, and in his people who reflect the holy one.

Fill thou my life, O Lord my God…
So shall no part of day or night
from sacredness be free,
but all my life, in every step,
be fellowship with thee.

TO PONDER

What are some things that tend to fill our life?

A CRIPPLED WOMAN
LUKE 13: 10-17

There were so many people on that Sabbath
to hear the famous Rabbi teach, they obscured
her view, for she was like a birch tree branch
bent toward earth to stay, after a harsh winter's ice storm:
her eyes saw only robes and sandals,
for she could not straighten up.
She seldom ventured forth into the busy streets;
the humiliation cut deep into Abraham's daughter
when bored boys would jeer and mock her insignificance,
and even grownups failed to greet the one
they'd honored as their friend and neighbor
eighteen years ago, when she still stood tall among them,
before an evil spirit bent what once was straight.

But she had come this day to hear him speak,
of whom her children had talked so much:
his words of wisdom, truth, compassion
her heart was hungry for.
She had no expectations that she'd feel the Rabbi's touch
or even see his face in the crowded synagogue;
it was enough to be near where he stood
and be encouraged by his words.
But when the needy come into his presence,
the unexpected becomes the norm.

When the Rabbi called to her to come to him,
she, now Spirit-driven, did not hesitate,
but shuffled forward and tried to raise her eyes to see his face.
In his eyes she saw his love,
and from his mouth she heard the words:
"Woman, be free from your infirmity."
His hands were gentle when he touched her,

but the power surging through her spine
potent enough to make the crooked straight.
Then the praise of God burst from her lips
as she walked erect past indignant worshipers,
her life forever altered by the Christ.

Oh Lord, you sought no adulation of the masses,
yet the masses gathered everywhere,
you came in fleshly weakness and with
the meekness of a lamb, but the Word
and power and love of God were evident to all.
They brought the blighted lives of lepers and deranged,
they brought the crippled, paralyzed, and blind,
as we would bring all those among us who are ill,
and a hundred others who pray for wholeness every day.

Dear Lord, though your earthly journey's done,
touch these needy lives in your compassion,
may they know the presence of the Son,
and the lasting joy of your redemption.

⌒ TO PONDER ⌒
**Is anyone "crippled" among those
you love personally?**

PRAYING

God, do our many prayers ever make you sick?

I don't mean the number of them so much, although having trouble myself listening to more than one conversation or speech at a time, I do wonder at that. But I'm quite content to ascribe that to one of your Godly attributes.

I think I mean more of the nature of so many of our prayers. We make a ritual of it. Many of our prayers function like a chairperson's gavel that calls the meeting to order. In Christian churches and schools, meetings aren't "official" unless "opened" —and often "closed"—with prayer.

Did your Son pray at the wedding in Cana? Did he open the Sermon on the Mount with prayer? Did Jesus "say grace" before dinner at Levi's house? Or at Mary and Martha's?

I know he taught the disciples—and us—about prayer:

> *Don't be like the hypocrites who love to pray in public places for effect. Don't babble like pagans who think they'll be heard because of their many words.*
>
> *Go into your private room when you pray, and close the door.*
> *Jesus got up early in the morning, left the house, and went off to a solitary place, where he prayed.*

I'm wondering about your point of view, God. Do you hear many of our prayers as little clichéd speeches we say to each other? Do you see us often listening to these prayers with our heads, if at all, rather than joining our hearts to them? Is it true that for many of us these "public" prayers take the place of our private ones? Do many of our prayers stink like odious sacrifices in your nostril, God?

I know, Father, you want your children to pray. And I know that as your children we need to pray. Children who don't talk to their parents will lose them. But children who substitute platitudes or canned refrains for meaningful communication will lose them too.

We want to talk to you, Lord. We want to shout hallelujahs to you when our life overflows with grace. We want to whimper our fears to you when we feel so vulnerable, so alone. We want to share our soul struggles with you at the Jabbok junctures of our life. We want to plead with you for the wellbeing of a friend or son. And you're right, Lord, for that we need to find our private place for prayer, a place where we keep no secrets.

Dear God, teach us to pray.

TO PONDER

What do *you* think about "public prayers"?

A Prayer for the Future

(Note: much of the language for this prayer comes from the NIV Bible)

O Lord, let us be still and know that you are God.

We want to trust in the future.
We want to say to our possessions: "You are my security."
We want to cling to our health and those we love.
But we know that all these things are fragile; they are like a
     spider's web,
like a fleeting shadow that does not endure.
For you, O Lord, have made our days a mere handbreadth.
Therefore teach us to number our days.

We know too well that life can be hard sometimes:
Terrors can overwhelm, dignity can be driven away as by the
     wind, safety can vanish like a cloud.
O Lord, when our harp is tuned to mourning and our flute to the
     sound of wailing,
then listen to our cry for help; then be not deaf to our weeping;
then may your unfailing love come to us, O God;
then may our Shepherd-God find his lost sheep and carry us
     safely home;
then may we remember that you have engraved us on the palms
     of your hands;
then may our soul seek God and find rest in him,
for our hope comes from him.

Lord, we spend most of our lives foolishly storing up treasures
     on earth.
Let us not forget the wisdom of the Preacher:
It's better to have a meal of vegetables where there is love than a
     fattened calf with hatred.
If the love of money is the root of all kinds of evil, Lord,
then help us to honor you with our wealth and with all our gifts:

by reaching out to the poor who are drenched by mountain rains
and hug the rocks for lack of shelter,
by rescuing those who cry for help, by spending ourselves on
behalf of the hungry,
by opposing those who make unjust laws, who deprive the poor
of their rights
and withhold justice from the oppressed,
by breaking the power of evil men who make friends with the
terror of darkness
that rapes and maims and murders and destroys all that God
called good,
by giving clothes to the naked, by giving aid to the fatherless
who have none to assist them,
by making the widow's heart sing, by being eyes to the blind and
feet to the lame,
by giving strength to the weary and increasing the power
of the weak.
Lord, may we be rich in good deeds for the love of God
and neighbor.

O God, you've made this world so beautiful!
Surely the heavens declare the glory of God:
when he spreads out the northern skies over empty space,
when he suspends the earth over nothing,
when he wraps the water in his clouds, when he covers the face
of the full moon,
when he marks out the horizon on the face of the waters for a
boundary between light and darkness,
when by his power he churns up the sea, when by his breath the
skies become fair!
We're but beginning to comprehend a little of the vast expanses
of the universe.
We cannot bring forth the constellations in their season,
nor can we tip over the water jars of the heavens
when the dust becomes hard and the clods of earth
stick together.

Yet we've used our puny power too often to deface the beauty of
    your creation,
we have too often dishonored the Creator by destroying or
    neglecting what he entrusted to our care.
Help us, Lord, to take more care for nature and its creatures,
even as we vow to take more care for each other,
for the earth and all its fullness is the Lord's.
In the midst of that fullness, Lord, help us to live in simplicity of
    spirit and lifestyle,
finding delight in all that is good and beautiful, cultivating
    relationships
that intensify our love for God, for his world, and for each other.

O God, in the years of this new century before us, send forth
    your light and your truth, let them guide us.
Make wars to cease to the ends of the earth; break the bows
and shatter the spear; burn the shields with fire.
Uphold all those who fall, lift up all who are bowed down, watch
    over all who love you.
You have promised that you will never leave us, that you will
    never forsake us,
and so we say with confidence that the Lord is our helper; we
    will not be afraid.
May we experience, Lord, that your compassion never fails,
that your mercy is new every morning, for great is your
    faithfulness!
O Lord, give us to know that our Redeemer lives
and that in the end we will see him with our own eyes,
and the yearning of our heart will at last be satisfied.

O Lord, let us be still and know that you are God.

IF I WERE A PREACHER

If I were a preacher, Lord, I would compel the crowds to come
and listen.

Surrounded by the multitudes, I would hold them spellbound
with the drama of life in which God is on center stage,
unnoticed by most players.

With the power of a George Whitefield and a Billy Graham,
power as a gift of grace, I would spark revivals on widely
scattered continents.

Everywhere the crowds would come.

And with the color and intensity of a Dwight Moody sermon, I
would lay on them the claims of the Gospel.

Sometimes I would have them roar with laughter, the way
Charles Spurgeon could.

Sometimes I would have their faces grow thoughtful as I would
quietly and logically explicate God's truth, the way John
Wesley could.

But always my aim would be, as it was and is of all great
preachers, not the adulation but the transformation of the
listener.

If I were a preacher, Lord, not before super bowl-size crowds in
the stadiums of the world, but in an ordinary pulpit of an
ordinary congregation, my aim would still be the same.

I would preach as a dying man to dying men and women.

No empty exhortations about the impossible, or rambling
reiterations of the too familiar.

No. I would tell stories, true stories, and stories of truth.

I would incite the imagination.

I would make my people laugh and weep with me.

I would open their minds and hearts to the mystery and majesty
and mercy of Immanuel—God with us.

Informed by wide-ranging reading and inspired by profound
meditation, I would make vivid to my congregation, to
young and old, the implications of Immanuel for our lives as

persons, as congregations, as communities, as citizens of a
shrinking, fragile world.

To ears in danger of deafness by the trivia of the entertainment
media, I would preach the penetrating challenge of making
Immanuel visible to blinded eyes, of making Him visible in
our homes and schools and market places and government
assemblies, and in a thousand other places where His
presence must make the difference.

The power of such preaching would come from God's own Word,
made alive through the ministry of the Spirit, so that—as it
did for Martin Luther—its feet would run after and its hands
would lay hold of every reader, of every listener.

For it must finally be the power of the Gospel that will make
people say, after the preaching, "I will do something."

But I'm not preacher, Lord, not even Rev. Walter Mitty.

And if I were a preacher, not just in fantasy but in a real place
and to real people, I would more likely be quickly sobered by
my limited gifts that would hardly be commensurate with the
unlimited expectations of my parishioners.

I might often suffer a sense of failure, not of the Gospel, but
because of sermons that didn't connect, illustrations that fell
flat, points that were misunderstood, unsanctified lives that
remained unchanged.

I might often grow weary from petty details and petty people and
an 80-hour workweek.

I might often suffer frustration and depression from an inability
to do justice to theological study, to remaining informed on
current literature and life, to the problems of my parishioners,
to the needs of my family.

But I'm not a preacher, Lord.

I suffer neither from a preacher's delusion of grandeur nor from
his nightmare of despair.

Like most of us, I just listen to them.

And often, I think about them.

About the pitfalls of success; about the pit of failure and low
self-esteem.

About our raised expectations and lowered estimations of
preachers today.

About the media-age pressures to perform in the pulpit rather
than to testify.

About their need of our prayers, our words of encouragement,
our acts of love.

But especially about our mutual need: to find joy in Him who has
redeemed us and called us to His service in the early years of
the twenty-first century.

Then preachers and parishioners, possessed by holy joy, can
worship together in ways that edify, that inspire, that nurture
the faith and strengthen the resolve to be our Lord's faithful
witnesses.

To your glory, God.

ON THE HOT SEAT

Hot seats are found in many places:
court rooms, dentist chairs, a doctor's office,
employment agencies, even classroom desks.
To be in the hot seat gives anxiety,
for it says you're in need of something,
or that you need to prove yourself.

The church has a hot seat too,
where elders meet to hear those led
to profess their faith in Jesus Christ.
Most come with a sense of trepidation,
for it's not a trivial occasion:
the integrity of one's faith is on the line,
though we know that the ultimate judge
of one's profession is you, our God,
who also sees the heart.

Would it not be good for all of us
to occupy that hot seat once again
ten years later, twenty, or fifty,
and answer the basic questions
we were asked at the time of our profession:

"What does Jesus mean to you?
What does it mean to be a member of Christ's Church?
How important is the Church to you?
How important is Bible reading to you?
Do you often pray alone?
How is your faith integrated in your daily life?
What does it mean to 'take up your cross'?"

It's a blessing to hear the young of faith
speak to such searching questions.
It's a blessing to encourage their commitment
and pray for their fruitfulness.

It's a blessing too to see oneself again on that hot seat
and give our answers silently before you, God.
A blessing to discover where we've fallen short,
and a blessing to affirm that Jesus is our Lord.

⟶ TO PONDER ⟵
**Would *you* respond differently to the
"basic questions" *now*?**

SPIRIT-SOARING TIMES

There are special times that make our spirit soar:
spring's first crocus, a first date, the birth of a child,
the rising rim of an early morning sun,
the fullness of a harvest moon hanging
like a ripened pumpkin low on the horizon,
sunsets, snow-capped mountains mirrored in mile-deep lakes;
Handel's "Worthy is the Lamb,"
the haunting strains of Pachelbel's "Canon in D Major."

Your church, Lord, has such times too:
ordination, baptisms, communion, acceptance letters,
Christmas morning, Easter sunrise service, and wedding vows.

But what a very special time when one stands up
in the midst of the congregation
to profess her faith in Jesus Christ the Lord.

Let us never, Lord, allow such sacred moments to become
commonplace, perfunctory, an impersonalized ritual,
or a mere interruption in the regular liturgy.
Let the whole church soar in communal celebration
of faith, hope, and the love of God.

SHARING
OUR FAITH

We do not live in an Age of Faith.

Venturing out, as we must, we encounter assaults more than affirmations of our faith.

We encounter strugglers more than heroes of the faith.

Sometimes we find ourselves in the company of a Jacob and Moses and David and Job and Jonah and Thomas and Peter.

Sometimes their struggle is ours.

Then we pray for faith to steady us, to reconnect us, to redirect us.

Faith not as a private possession but as a public practice.

Faith not to be hoarded but shared.

CHURCH AND FOUNDATIONS

We were walking across the university campus one summer
 morning, on the way to our seminar.
I don't remember now how the subject came up.
But what she said still sticks with me: "I lost my faith when
 Martin Luther King was shot. When I went to church that
 week, I heard a sweet, disgusting sermon about love.
I haven't been to church since."

There was bitterness in Carol's voice, Lord.
She had lost much: her church, her faith, such as it was, and
 later on her marriage too.
I felt her hurt, her sense of loss, and I was pained then, as I am
 still, that the church failed.

I'm thinking now of other friends, a couple eager for parenthood.
They prayed hard, and they found their cup running over when
 Joy became pregnant.
When Alicia was born, they discovered the serious defects.
But they loved their little girl with all their heart.
Their heart broke when after six months precious baby Alicia
 died.
They lashed out at the God who had given and then, cruelly,
 taken.
The foundation of their faith began to crumble.
And their church kept silent.

Yes, Lord, I know the church is human too.
It's sadly true that the people in the pew and the preacher in the
 pulpit do sometimes cause weak ones to stumble.
For there are many Carols and Joys whose faith can be so
 vulnerable, so tentative, even conditional.
They come to church for spiritual moorings.
They hover, on the periphery of the faithful, eager for negation
 of their doubts, eager for affirmation of their hopes, eager for
 reassurance in a world that nurtures fear and cynicism, eager

for fuller revelation to establish a foundation of faith on rocks
that can survive the storms.
They are in search of you, oh God.
Thus they are quick to spot the weakness and failures of
the church.
They look for harmony but find strife and dissension.
They look for sincerity but find superficiality and hypocrisy.
They look for love but find gossip and ill-will.
They look for the support and grace of compassion but find
withdrawal.
They scrutinize and judge our words and actions, and often fail
to find what their spirits seek.
Bewildered and betrayed, they withdraw, often never to
come back.

In penitence, oh Lord, we pray, forgive us, and give us zeal
to make through us, your Church, the Gospel real.

☙ TO PONDER ☙
Have *you* met a Carol or a Joy in *your* life?

DROPOUTS

I know some people who no longer go to church.
They've dropped out
like indifferent runners from a race.
Some have dropped their faith too
like excess baggage no longer needed or wanted
or like a garment that no longer fits
reluctantly parted with.
(Haunt them, Lord.)

Some hang on to faith
but found it violated in their church
and, bruised and battered, left
betrayed and bitter.
(Heal them, Lord.)

I'm grateful for my faithful church
where the Thomas and the Peter
surfacing so easily
have been rebuked
by seeing faith in action through burdens shared
and much good work with gladness done.
(Thank you, Lord.)

The faithful and the wavering need a church
where love and sympathy can grow
when fellow members hurt
and grief becomes too much to bear alone
where grace is visible
in quiet acts of kindness, courage, peace,
through words and gestures
that convey Immanuel.
(Teach us, Lord.)

> *You are one body in Christ*
> *members of one another*

love each other
be patient in tribulation
be constant in prayer
rejoice with those who rejoice
weep with those who weep
live at peace with all.

QUESTIONS

Lord, there are questions we have often heard.
We hear them still, with new ones added now and then.
Questions that haunt us, perplex us, and keep us humble.
For we don't know the answers to most of them.

Did God come from nowhere, at no time?

Where did we come from in the beginning?
Where do we end up at the end?
Will we really live forever after we die?
What will we be doing?
Will we have free will? Do we have it now?

Why are we not all born equal?
Will we all be equal in heaven?
But not the same?

What is the purpose of evil in the world?
How was evil born before the beginning?
How will it be prevented in the hereafter?

Why did God place the tree with the forbidden fruit in
    the Garden?

Did God create us in his image,
or do we try to create him in ours?

Is it possible to truly adore the Creator but abuse the creation?
Is it possible to truly love our children but let them feed on the
    hollow values of our culture?
Must we really make this a better world for those who come
    after us?

Is our sexuality God's gift or God's joke?
Or is it we that make a joke of God's gift?
Why does the sun shine on both the evil and the good?

Did God really love Jacob but hate Esau?
Why do "acts of God" strike so indiscriminately?

Who's in control?
Was God, when millions were murdered in gas chambers?
Or slain in the Gulag?
Or vaporized (and maimed) one sunny day in Hiroshima?
Is God, when we let millions starve or be aborted?
Or when a lover, in a fit of jealous rage, kills your only daughter?
If God doesn't pull the strings, do we do it ourselves?

Why are there so many singles looking for marriage partners, but
    never find one?
Why do so many marriages fail?
Why do some couples pray for children but never get them,
while others get more than is good for them?

Do ALL things really work together for good...? Always?

Why is God so silent?
Why doesn't God prove to all that he exists?

Can we be truly happy when we hear voices nearby or far away
crying for bread, for work, for justice, for dignity, for hope?

Why is it easier to be generous when we have little than when
    we have much?
Why is it so hard to accept charity, even God's ?

Why is it all right to kill when in military uniform?

Can there be forgiveness without repentance?
    Grace without guilt?
O Lord, there are so many questions we have no answer to.

But there's no question in my mind about this:
When Paula comes in each Sunday morning with needy Tim
    and Saralee,
I know the Lord is coming in too.

When Janet Rose, nearly consumed by cancer,
sits and sings and prays among us, I know God is there right
    beside her.
When Bob De Haan wages his desperate battle for life
with yet another round of chemo, I know his hand is holding on
    to yours.
When these men visit Jim Wallace every Thursday night,
it's out of the love you placed inside their hearts.
When Doris Smith submits once again to a 20-hour plane ride,
to long hours of hard work in often difficult conditions,
it's your call she couldn't reject.
When Tom Sterk speaks for the poor and weak and needy,
I hear the voice of God;
when he works to bring shalom,
I see the work of God.

Our questions won't go away anytime soon, Lord.
Sometimes they crowd in on us, insistent like the ring of
    our alarm.
They're good to raise, to ponder, and to share.
But don't let them blind our eyes or stop our ears to "God
    with us."
Don't let them make us doubt that we too, each of us,
broken vessels though we are, can be used by the Master
to show God to each other, and to our world.

Use us, Lord; use even me.

⌒ TO PONDER ⌒
What's the biggest question in *your* life?

PROFESSING THE FAITH

I made a commitment, Father.
Your Spirit led me to say that I'll take up my cross
and follow you.
Now the pilgrim road lies ahead.
I'm eager to travel that road, Lord.
But I'm a little afraid too.
I know sometimes the travel will be easy,
when good friends and family are all around
to laugh and talk and be with me.
I love those times, Lord,
when I feel close to people
and when I feel close to you,
times when the world seems so full of
goodness and joy and beauty
that it's easy to be kind and decent,
easy to praise and serve and love you.

But even those times scare me a little, Lord.
When life is sweet and success is constant,
when family is loving and friends are close,
when blood flows strong inside my veins
and there's almost nothing that I lack—
then, Father, let me not forget you.
In the happy bustle of my living
don't let me lose sight of the Giver.
May your place never be diminished by
people or power or possessions or pleasure.
Even when life is filled to the brim with good things,
press the cross and the yoke upon me
as reminders of whom I must have first in life.

I know there will be other times as well, dear Lord.
Times when those I loved and needed
are taken away.

Times when my hopes and prayers
turn to heartaches and to tears.
Times when I grow afraid and weary,
when I feel alone, estranged, confused,
a forsaken pilgrim on a lonely road.
Then, yes, especially then, Oh Lord,
take my hand and lead me on.

When the road takes sudden twists and turns,
keep me steady, Lord.
When I sight along the way the grotesque figures
and actions of those who are demonized,
save me from cynicism and despair.

When I discover the unyielded places in my own heart,
the arid places I retained as private property,
then, Father, turn my shame into real penitence
and my hypocrisy into radical discipleship.

When life grows stale and purposefulness wanes,
when I am troubled and begin to lose my peace of mind,
then, Father, may your overwhelming presence
with peace and purpose fill my life again.

When grief and pain would tempt to bitterness,
may your healing grace descend
and turn my pain to prayer.

On this pilgrim road, dear Lord,
help me to love you
with all my heart and mind and strength,
help me to love my neighbor as myself.

⟿ TO PONDER ⟿
Do you think of yourself as a pilgrim?

FAITH

I pray for faith, Lord. It often proves elusive. Why does it have to
     be so hard?
Because I want to understand what I believe? Because I
     want proof?
Perhaps.
We've often been betrayed, learned to be skeptical about
     many things.
Still, I have a hunch that neither proof nor understanding
can produce the faith I long for—
the kind of faith that moves mountains of doubt and despair
     into the sea.

Not the kind of faith that turns men into demons in God's name.
Not the accouterments of faith either: sending checks to charity,
going to church, visiting the sick,
stocking the food pantry, participating in Bible Study—
all the good and necessary things we do.

But faith, that permeates my being with your undeniable
     presence:
the faith of Enoch who "walked with God,"
the faith of Abraham who was ready to give back the son
for whom he waited all his life,
the faith of Moses who stepped into the Red Sea with Pharaoh
     on his heels,
the faith of Rahab, so filled with the sense that
"the Lord your God is God in heaven above and on the
     earth below"
that she risked her life by helping the spies escape,
the faith of Joseph when he took the pregnant Mary as his wife,
the faith of Mary when she stepped among the stable's animals
to give birth to your Son,
the faith of Anna who never gave up hope of seeing the Messiah,
the faith of Peter when he stepped over the boat's railing
into the roiling water to meet Jesus.

O Lord, I want the faith of such unlikely men and women as the
    centurion,
an officer in the enemy occupation force,
of the lowly leper,
of that nobody in a pushy crowd who reached out her hand in
    faith to touch your cloak,
of the blind man,
of that no-count Canaanite woman who believed your crumbs
to be as potent as the bread,
of that embarrassing prostitute who, in polite company,
    slobbered all over your feet.
None had attended Christian School or studied theology.
Perhaps none had practiced the discipline of prayer.
But all made profession of their faith,
its impulse leaping forth from them so simply and so profoundly
that you were astonished, touched, and moved to heal, grant,
    forgive, and bless.
All believed, because they had met the living God.
To that encounter, faith was their unrehearsed response.

That's the faith you're looking for, in me, in all of us.
And that's the faith I want, I need.
Faith not as product of my understanding or intellect,
but faith that serves my intellect and yields understanding.
Faith not as an act of will, but faith that activates my will to
    Godly work.

In the years ahead, O God, lead me to divine encounters,
though our world in so many hearts and places
is void of faith and hope and charity.
In a world groaning for redemption, lead us all to meet the God
who is still present among the Roman legions,
among the lepers and the blind,
the rejects of Canaan and the prostitutes.
And when we meet you, God, in strange places,
or in the neighborhood, our work, our friends,
may our faith ignite and change us forever.

Even when wars darken the sky, may our hope not waver,
even when we lose what we value dearly, may our love not cease.

For your faith has made you whole.

☞ TO PONDER ☜
Is your faith making *you* whole?

CONFLICTED GRATITUDE

"Let your hearts overflow with thankfulness," said Paul.

Well, I think I'm having trouble with gratitude.

Oh, I have moments of brimming over,
the heart too full with thanks
for a gesture or a word of kindness,
for a touch of love that's holy,
for a glimpse of beauty so palpable
you think you're looking through
a window into heaven,
for a sudden sense of nearness to God
that suffuses everything with glory.

These come mostly, God, as your unbidden
and unexpected gifts of grace:

> someone saying "your prayer blessed me today";
> small arms suddenly, spontaneously around your neck
> and a voice whispering in your ear, "I love you, grandpa";
> a golden harvest moon rising over Grand Traverse Bay,
> or a scooped-out valley near its shore with its grove
> of fall-splashed trees shimmering under the early
>   morning sun.

Still, my life is not a constant litany of praise.
For some of us have more than others, and when I look
at those whose burdens look much larger than their blessings,
I feel they need my prayer more than you need my praise
for all that's good and right with me.
Then my moments of grateful adoration often turn into
contending with a God of inequalities.
It's the all-night struggle at the Jabbok that still engages
me more than the green pastures where sheep do safely graze.

Serenity eludes me in a world where beasts of prey
transform green pastures into bloody killing fields.

Dear Lord, I want to revel more
in all that's Godly, good, and gracious,
even when I smell the sewers
and see the fissures of this broken world.

ISAIAH 61

Dear God, we are your singers on this earth
    we sing of peace and joy and light
    we bring glad tidings of new birth
to all who cry and suffer in the night.

We sing to those afflicted and in grief
    we lift the brokenhearted ones
    we sing of love, hope, and relief,
of restored lives and blessed innocence.

We sing to those chained in a prison cell
    the ancient prophet's freedom song
    we sing deliverance from hell
to all the lost who for salvation long.

We sing, we shout for all the world to hear:
    take off your rags, put on the new
    night has ended, the Lord is near
all God's promises will at last come true!

Therefore we sing from sea to shining sea
    with steadfast faith and holy mirth
    let's clear away the last debris
and let's begin to build our God's new earth.

SIDES

We wonder, Lord: on whose side are you?
Are you liberal or conservative?
Are you for women preachers and acceptance of gays?

We'd like to know that, Lord.
It would make things so much easier.
Synods could simply chant: "Who is on the Lord's side..."
And delegates could start lining up, on one side or the other.

As, of course, they already do.
Trouble is, they all think they are on your side.
Who's right and who's wrong?
Neither?
Both?

We all line up, of course.
Some on the side of Truth and Tradition.
Surely, that's the right side.
Or will you indict them with limited understanding and
    dead orthodoxy?

Some on the side of Equality and Justice.
Surely those are godly principles.
Or will you question the purity of their zeal and the practice of
    their principles?

Some insist, Lord, that you made the cosmos
by human clock time in roughly 72 hours, and not so very
    long ago.
Some point to findings that lead to very different conclusions.
Thus Christian brothers and sisters glare at each other and think
    unholy thoughts.
All say that this world belongs to God,
that they live to serve you,
that they mean to keep the Great Commandments.

Yet love for God and neighbor so quickly dissipates
into unrighteous indignation and mutual rejection.

Lord of the Church, how weighty are these issues on your
    Kingdom scales?
Ought they to consume us?
Ought they to fragment your Church?
Show us, Lord, your side, that we may reflect more of your
    presence in this world.
Show us, Lord, and we will follow by God's grace.

*Live in harmony with one another...love as brothers and sisters, be
compassionate and humble...do not repay insult with insult...seek
peace and pursue it...go and make disciples....*

⟶ TO PONDER ⟵
Is it possible to show love to one you disagree with?

Sunday School

As children we love to hear the words from parents and Sunday
school teachers:

God loves you and will never let anything bad happen to you.
Don't be afraid, God will not let the Devil hurt you.
Nothing happens without the will of your Father.
God will answer your prayer and give you all that's good.

In the scary world of childhood, those words wrap themselves
around us as if they are your almighty arms, and we feel
secure. Before we fall asleep at night, we whisper, "Thank
you, Lord, for taking care of me."

We grow up with some confidence that it shall be so. For we've
learned that you, our God, are strong and infinitely good.
You're our Father who has called us precious in his sight.
Surely, we're in good hands that will not let us go where we
can fall.

Yet we know that Adam and Eve were banished from
the Garden
that Cain killed Abel, that Tamar was violated by an
evil brother
that Uriah was killed on the battle front, the victim of
insidious treachery
by the chosen one of God
that the innocent babes in Bethlehem were murdered
that John the Baptist was beheaded through the rashness of
a sotted fool
that Stephen was stoned by a Christ-hating mob

And we remember
that one of our members was shot dead when she was
still a teen

that another teen was burned like trash when she was
    searching for Home
that a beloved son drowned when life glowed bright
    with promise
that a daughter lost her legs when trying to help others
that a thirteen-year old's brilliant smile suddenly froze into
    the mask of death
that a colleague was killed by cancer when so many good
    years were still supposed to come
that a friend was struck down by debilitating MS when he
    wasn't finished playing and wrestling with his kids
that the refugee in our midst lost both her father and mother
    to violent death when she was hardly old enough to
    remember them

and there are more, so many more....

Often sooner than later, we discover or experience that bad
    things happen to good people all the time; and all the lessons
    of our youth explode in our face.
Often our faith does too. We are bewildered and feel betrayed.

Oh, help us, God, not to tell lies to the young; help us not to
    believe them ourselves:
You may not keep bullets or disease or accidents or death far
    from us.

You may not keep us from losing a child or spouse.

You may not protect us from abuse nor a child from going astray.

You may not save us from the indignities of old age.

You may not give us all we ask for.

We're not the prophet Elijah, not even the apostle Peter.

You are not our personal body guard or magician or servant.

But you have shown us how frail and fleeting is our life.

Help us to remember, even as we bustle about,
heaping up our human chestnuts, ignorant of who shall
    get them.

With David we pray, "Lord, make me to know my end.

Hear my prayer, O Lord, listen to my cry for help; 'be not deaf to
    my weeping."

I take pity on the weak and needy.

Underneath are my everlasting arms.

I offer refuge in the shadow of my wings:
I hear your cry and send my love and faithfulness.

I have made you. Even to your old age and gray hairs,
I will sustain you.

Cast all your anxiety on me, because I care for you.

I will never leave you nor forsake you.

Thank you, Father. We believe; help us in our unbelief.

And let us never forget "What a Friend we have in Jesus."

⚘ TO PONDER ⚘
**How do *you* share your faith with good people who
suffer bad things?**

THE HOLY LIFE

When we're very young, we live in the present. Others, like our
     parents, if we're blessed, take care for and of the future.
But Lord, it was different for you.
Your mother and your Father knew about a destiny that like a
     sword would pierce hearts.

You were still a young boy when you chided your mother for not
     remembering that your purpose on earth was to be about
     your Father's business.
You knew even then your purpose for being born.

Had I known, at age 30 or far before, that my life would end
     violently before it had barely bloomed, nailed to a cross on
     Outcast Hill, what would I have done; how would I have lived?

Wallowed in self-pity? Stunned into immobility? Schemed
     endlessly to circumvent my fate?

Can life be "normal" when its end is known?
How plan a career, a marriage, a family when the only certainty
     is death at an early age?
Because death comes tomorrow, would I have tried to lose myself
     in eating and drinking and making merry?
Or would I have searched and longed with all my heart for the
     Comforter whose love is constant both in life and death?
Would I have bent my strength and spirit into making every
     day count for something that would last beyond my own
     short life?
Would I have lived with dull resignation or the spark of eternity
     in my eyes?

Search me, O God, and know my heart; test me and know my
     anxious thoughts.
See if there is any offensive way in me, and lead me in the way
     everlasting.

You knew that every step you took brought you closer to the
  agony of the Cross.
You knew it when you partied with the wedding guests at Cana.
And you knew it when you wept at the tomb of Lazarus.
But you reached out in one continuous gesture of serving bodies
  and souls:
You healed, you fed, you taught, you told earthly stories with
  heavenly meanings.
And you prayed, in the silence of the mountain, in the dark but
  quiet hours of the night,
and when the night turns liquid, just before the dawning of new
  light.
You talked with God.

It was not an easy life. But it was focused, for there was no time
  to waste.
It was a life of passionate commitment, holy intensity, and
  absolute integrity.
It was a life of giving: of your strength, your power, your
  compassion, and your love.
It was a life of living—and dying—for others.
And when at last you had given your very life, you said:
  It is done.

Dear Lord, we do not know the number of our days.
But thank you for showing us how to live.
Thank you for loving us, even unto death.
Thank you for saving us from our sinful ways,
and shaping us into a new creation
in Christ, our Lord.

TO PONDER
What's the "new creation" life like?

THE TEMPLE

That first journey to Jerusalem, Lord,
was it all and more than you had dreamed about?

Running around with friends from school and neighborhood,
the caravan steadily moving south toward David's City
through the springtime beauty of the land
green with young corn and vines and hills of olives,
at night singing the songs of Israel around camp fires,
and, tired at last, falling asleep under God's starry heaven—
this rite of passage, Lord, was it a highlight of your life?

And when near journey's end the roads grew thick with crowds
coming from the four corners of the land,
did parents warn their children to stay close
lest they get lost and miss Seder, the early evening feast?
And then, when you crested the last ridge of hills
and Jerusalem spread before you like a fairy tale,
did you beg to see the House of God, your Father, first
before pitching camp on the Mount of Olives slope—
this first trip away from home, was it like coming home?

Did you enter through Gate Beautiful, push your way
through narrow streets choked with pilgrims, hawkers, slaves
till the Temple rose before you on the Temple Mount,
its pinnacles gleaming golden in the bright Judean sun?
Did God's holy temple hush the crowd, or did the raucous
temple merchants and the money changers raise your ire
    even then?
And later, were you startled by the sounding of the shofar,
calling pilgrims to the ceremony of the sacrifice?
Did you help Joseph carry the unblemished lamb to the altar
and see its blood dashed against the base?
And when you observed the rituals of the Seder
with your people, shared the body of the lamb,

broke unleavened bread, and drank the bitter herbs—
did you feel the weight of its significance sink into your soul
    already then,
though the Last Supper in the Upper Room was very far away?

You discovered your preference for quiet places
far from the festive frenzy of the madding crowds
and found the Temple's quiet inner court
where learned rabbis taught the brightest of the young
about Yahweh and his people and his promise
of the Messiah, greater than Moses, who would come
with power to deliver Israel from its yoke.
You came, you listened, asked questions, talked
while they listened to the Word made flesh,
asked questions too and were amazed at your understanding
and your answers as you taught the masters at the age of twelve.
Already eager to exchange the father's carpenter shop
for the Father's temple, you were where you felt at home.

But your time had not yet come.
You returned to Nazareth with friends and family
who did not understand that the Father's business
was and would be waiting in Jerusalem.
Did you know then what they could not,
all that would pass between your first visit and the last:
three years of homeless wandering across arid deserts
and through dirty towns, among the riff-raff and the rich
and motley multitudes that needed healing and a word of hope?
Did you know then what they could not,
that on your last Passover pilgrimage, the place
where once your were honored as precocious youth,
would now betray and taunt and hang the Son of God
    for blasphemy?
Then, about your Father's business still,
you yourself would be the Lamb,
the God-man sacrifice to set God's people free.

And then you would be Home at last.
We, for whom you lived and died, now pray:
turn our faces to the New Jerusalem,
keep us focused on the Father's will
serving those we meet along the way
until we too shall lay our burden down,
and we shall hear you say:
welcome home, I have a place for you,
the old has passed away, look, I've made all things new.

ASCENSION

I've never seen a loved one go to heaven, Lord,
as the disciples did from that familiar spot
on the Mount of Olives where you had shown
and taught them much about another kingdom
they had hardly ever dreamed or thought about.
But now they saw you rise above all earthly kingdoms
and move beyond the things they saw and knew,
beyond their touch and voice and fellowship:
an awesome moment and a speechless one
to see one's loved one go where none can follow.
Yet when James and John and Peter and the rest
set their faces to Jerusalem, there was no God-forsaken feeling
but an angel's promise ringing in their ears:
As you have seen him go, so will he come again.

It's been two thousand years since then
though God's time counts a thousand years as one.
Still, we would pray with the repentant criminal:
Jesus, remember me now that you've come into your kingdom.
Remember me, when I mutter and mope and muddle my way
through the muck and mayhem of our time.
Remember me when branches lash my face
and cobwebs clog my hair because the world is not always
a neat and tidy place with highways going everywhere.
Remember me when I grow weak and I betray
the truth, the way, the life that never ends,
when I in blindness seek that which offends
your will and love for me.
Remember me and hear my cry
when the load gets heavy
and I want to put it down and die
before the road runs out.
Oh Lord, remember me!

Do not be afraid; I will not leave you as orphans.
Love me, then my Father will love you too,
and we will come to you and make our home with you.
You will be with me in paradise; I'm preparing a place for you.
I myself will raise you up on the last day.
Come to me, and I will give you rest.
Now let your light shine.
And show others that you are my disciples by loving one another.

⮞ TO PONDER ⮜
How do you show *your* discipleship?

ENOCH

"Oh for a closer walk with God," we sing.
It's a fine hymn to sing in church after a sermon on piety.
It's a fine old hymn to sing for family devotions at the
    dinner table.
They're splendid words to whisper in a bedtime prayer after
    a quiet hour
of spiritual reflection.

But Enoch did not have to sing about a closer walk with God.
He didn't even have to pray about it.
He did it.
That's what the Bible says: "Enoch walked with God."

And Enoch was no cloistered monk.
He did not sit in a secluded garden all day, communing with God.
All in all, he probably lived a pretty ordinary life, as far as most
    could tell.
He hung out with his friends. He fell in love.
He married, and his first-born son became the oldest man
    in history.
He had to make a living. He sweated and grunted as he tilled the
    cursed ground.
He played with his children, and with his children's children.
No doubt there came a time when he had trouble remembering
    the names
of all the descendants that kept coming after him.
Pity his oldest son, though, who outlived his daddy by some
    600 years!

Yes, Enoch lived among his people, and they thought he was just
    one of them.
But he was not.
For his was no ordinary life, and he was no ordinary man.
Enoch walked with God; for 365 days a year; for 365 years
    on earth.

And there's nothing ordinary about that.
"To walk with God"—what a beautiful expression of a
    relationship,
how inexhaustible its meaning.
Did You, his God, stroll with Enoch in the twilight
and in the cool breezes of a dewy dawn?
Somehow I doubt it, for Enoch did not live in Paradise.
But Enoch lived, I think, as if You were right there beside him,
    all the time.
And he must've felt comfortable with that presence, for he was
    in companionship.
You don't walk with someone you're afraid of or don't like,
with someone you don't trust or don't know what to say to.
No, you walk with someone because they're good company,
for mind and soul, as Enoch must've been for You, the Most
    High God!
Such good company, in fact, that You did not want to lose him:
at half the age of others, Enoch disappeared, for You took
    him away,
and thus Enoch walked with God into eternity.
Oh God, how great your love!

We'll keep singing, "Oh, for a closer walk with God."
Dear God, help us to do it too.
In peaceful nature walks, and quiet talks with spouse or friends,
but also in the midst of ringing phones and traffic jams,
of screaming kids and endless household chores,
help us to walk with God.

～ TO PONDER ～
How do *you* practice "a closer walk with God"?

WHERE ARE YOU?

"The man and his wife had hid themselves from the Lord among the trees of the Garden."

THE LORD GOD CALLED:
   "WHERE ARE YOU?"

None of your business. I wanta do what I wanta do, so don't bug me. I'm sick of everybody always bugging me—parents, teachers, even my little sister is trying to run my life. But I'm running it myself, just the way I want to. And what my friends and I do is our business. If we want to party, that's what we'll do. And if everybody wants to get high, we'll get high. Go away, leave me alone. First things first, my grandpa always says. Well, right now for me this is first.

THE LORD GOD CALLED:
   "WHERE ARE YOU?"

I'm busy. You know how competitive this world is. It takes all I've got to keep my head above water. Sure, I'm neglecting some things. I don't see my family much. I haven't had more than a five-minute talk with my wife for months. Personal devotions are non-existent. I don't suppose I can count the occasional "please God, let the profit curve go up a little higher this month!" I know, I know, there's the line about "gaining the whole world...." But I don't have time to think about that now. I'm often putting in an 18-hour day. I'm tired. Later, later I'll make it up. Get involved in church more. Work on my soul. Right now I'm buried under a mountain of business responsibilities. Yeah, I'm tired.

THE LORD GOD CALLED:
   "WHERE ARE YOU?"

Having the time of my life! I'm having a blast, really! I've got enough money to buy some toys now. I just made reservations for a condo at Vail for Christmas and New Year. We'll go with the whole family this year; that ought to make the kids happy! Ten years ago this was just a dream; now I have to pinch myself sometimes when I drive up to our Lake Michigan cottage in my Lexus, and see each of the kids have fun with their own jet ski instead of fighting over just the one we used to have; or when my wife and I take our good friends to a fine restaurant and think nothing of spending a hundred dollar bill. Yeah, God, you've sure been good to me. Success is sweet. I'm exactly where I want to be; it's like a piece of heaven now, and I hope I can stay there for a long time!

THE LORD GOD CALLED:
"WHERE ARE YOU?"

I think I'm lost, maybe forever. I'm not sure how it happened. Maybe I went into hiding, and then I got lost. I've heard you calling. I still do sometimes. But I'm afraid that one day I won't hear your voice at all. Because something deep inside my soul still wants to come, wants to find the path where you're waiting, wants to take your hand and walk with you. But I hold back. Maybe it's fear, fear of commitment. I don't mind going through the motions, for I also fear the opinion of others. But a going-all-out kind of commitment, that's frightening. That means change, and I'm not sure I want to change. To knock self off the throne and yield wholly to another—I just can't do it. Still, sometimes that's exactly what I want to do. Sometimes, when I ache for the peace that passes understanding, I want you to yank me out of the jungle of my retreat and force me to follow you. But that's not your way with me. I have to seek and I have to knock. And then I have to give—my heart and my will. O Lord, have mercy!

THE LORD GOD CALLED:
"WHERE ARE YOU?"

LOOKING FOR THE LORD

I've been looking for you, Lord.

> *Look for me in the hearts of the humble.*

I tried to find you at Synod where pious
people come to do the work of the church—
which we call your body. I heard them
quote and read from the same Bible;

> *Look for me in the lives of those who pray*
> *in the spirit and try earnestly*
> *to live their prayers.*

I heard them sing the same songs together.
But they were not of one mind.
There was no unity of the body.
I did not find you there.

> *Look for me in those who have*
> *suffered injustice and bear no bitterness.*

I've tried to find you in the churches
where folk in council rooms do "your will"
 by wielding their divine authority
to dictate, to tear asunder,
to have their way. They serve
themselves and feel righteous.
I did not find you there.

> *Look for me among those who really*
> *do love their neighbor as themselves.*
> *Look for me in the anguished faces of*
> *those who have lost a home, a job,*
> *a spouse, a child.*

I've tried to find you at the political
conventions where national leaders
invoke your name; where banner-waving,
slogan-spouting party members claim you

as cheerleader and vilify the opposition.
I did not find you there.

>Look for me in the desperate eyes of
>those who are dying the slow death
>of starvation.

>Look for me in the empty pocketbook
>of those who were rich and gave all
>to the poor.

Where are you, Lord? Where is your power
to expose the self-deceptions and vanity
of humankind?

>Look for me in the loneliness of those
>who feel like aliens in a foreign land.

I see the power of your creation to blow to
rubble whole human communities. Where is
your power to prevent destruction,
to bless the lives of frail creatures?

>I inhabit the wind-swept hollows of
>the human hearts. I scuttle around the
>edges of desperation and despair.
>I creep inside the cracks of failure.
>I enter the places of poverty.

>If you seek me there,
>you will surely find me.

Where are you, Lord? Where is your presence
that announces the kingdom of God with us,
that empowers your church to be light against
the kingdom of darkness?

>**Where are you?**

FAMILY LIFE

What counts for us in family life maybe more than all else
is our children.
We want their health and their happiness.
We want their success in school.
We want them to have good friends.
We want them spared from cruel words and deeds.
We want them to grow up honest and kind.
We want them to grow in favor with others and God.

We want so much for our children; that's why parents
pray a lot.
We pray for our own and for other children.
Because we know many children suffer—
from neglect, from unhappy home life, from peer pressure
and from a hundred other ills that distort or quench their
spirit.

We strive to grow strong the bonds between parent and
child.
We care when they hurt and celebrate when they achieve.
We listen to their stories, and we lead them in the way they
should go.
And one day we discover that they are grown, eager to go
out on their own.
And then we pray for grace to let them go.
And when they go, we let them know, our prayers will
always follow them.

SCHOOL TIME

Mother Mary shivers in the chill of early dawn,
hesitant to let go of her first-born's hand,
hesitant to release this special one
to the stern discipline of another teacher,
as all mothers are.

But Jesus starts school today.

Walking back through the narrow streets
of Nazareth, back to their home and work,
Joseph's head fills with thoughts of tasks and tools,
while Mary wonders whether in heaven
the Father's plans for his only Son
match her earthly dreams.

Do you remember, Jesus, when your little fingers
traced the Hebrew letter of the alphabet?
And when the letters from the Torah
turned into words, words into phrases,
did the word of Father Yaweh
become engravened on your soul:
"Hear, O Israel: the Lord our God is one Lord!"

But no one said, "Immanuel,"
And it was not yet time for him above
to tell the world with pride and love:
"This is my beloved Son
in whom I am well pleased."

But I think your teachers were:
as you memorized the sacred scriptures
and wise men's apt interpretations;
as you, later in the *bet talmud,*
the "house of learning," learned to

test your wits against their baits and traps,
to sift and weigh, and challenge
what could be supported by the evidence
within the scripture or the reason of lesser minds;
as your imagination flowered and you learned
how truth is told through fiction
of human tales and parables;
as your spirit soared through the poetry
of the Psalms and of the prophets;
as you confronted moral heroes and
evil's power to corrupt, and saw that
only God's authority is absolute;
as you were touched by those who're weak—
the poor, the homeless, the orphan, and the stranger,
and knew how you would spend your life and why.

In this new school season of the year, Lord,
our children—and your children too—
gather them all, we pray, with joy and laughter,
with tears too when compassion fills their hearts,
with love for learning, and a holy passion
to be children of the light in this shadow land.

Then parents, profoundly grateful, will exclaim:
"This is my beloved, growing in stature,
and in favor with others and with God."

PARENTING

We call you our Father; some call you our Mother.
And you are both a Father and a Mother to us, your children.
That's why we feel free to talk to you about parenting.
You have a lot of children, and quite a variety of them.
And we know that they haven't all been easy.
You've scolded and pleaded.
You've warned and you've wept.
You've cared about all of them, and still do.

You know how much we care about ours.
They fill us with that warm flow of love
when as infants we cradle them in our arms,
when we bend over their cribs
and watch them sleeping the sleep of innocence.
We love our kids, when they read their first book
and when they violate a curfew;
when they curl up on our lap
and when they bring home their first traffic ticket.
They're our children, regardless,
and we love them.

> *Children are a reward from the Lord. (Ps. 127:3)*

Yes, and we thank you for that special gift.
We want to take good care of them.
Maybe that's why they preoccupy us so much,
that's why we sometimes find ourselves distracted,
staring at something but only seeing our child,
his vulnerability exposed and needing our protection;
her willfulness leading her astray and needing our correction.

> *Be careful or you will be enticed to turn*
> *away and worship other gods*
> *and bow down to them. (Deut. 11:16)*

That's what worries us, Lord.
There are so many voices all around them:
voices that tempt with hollow promises,
voices of mindless conformity,
voices of doubt and cynicism,
voices of faith in glitter and glory.
Are they going to hear you, Lord?
And are they going to listen?

> *...be careful, and watch yourselves closely*
> *so that you do not forget the things your*
> *eyes have seen or let them slip from your heart*
> *as long as you live.*
> *Teach them to your children*
> *and to their children after them. (Deut. 4:9)*

Yes, Lord, yes.
But what a responsibility!
To be honest
(and before you, how could we pretend?),
we fail dismally at times.
Sometimes our children show us disrespect and anger us,
sometimes we fear they're up to no good
but we prefer not to deal with it.

> *The rod of correction imparts wisdom.*
> *Discipline your children*
> *and they will bring delight to your soul. (Prov. 29)*

Help us, Lord, to do that wisely
and not as a mere assertion of authority.
Help us to do that lovingly,
and not in a fit of temper.

> *...do not exasperate your children. (Ephes. 6:4)*

Thank you, Father,
for teaching us about being good parents.
We do love our children,
and we care about them very much.
We want to enjoy them,
to show them our care for them,
to be a good example,
to encourage them in the right
and to save them from the wrong.
Help us to do and to be what our children need most.
For Jesus' sake.

> Love the Lord your God
> with all your heart
> and with all your soul
> and with all your strength.
> These commandments...
> are to be upon your hearts.
> Impress them upon your children.
> Talk about them when you sit at home
> and when you walk along the road,
> when you lie down
> and when you get up. (Deut. 6)

⸿ TO PONDER ⸿
What do *your* children need most from you?

ADELINA

Dear Lord,

I'm used to be being back in school by now. (I think my mommy was glad when school started again. At first she kept saying how much she loved me. I noticed that she went to the library to get some books for herself.)

I'm pretty happy in school. I mean, I like the teacher and I have fun with my friends. But I want you to know about Adelina. She's in my class. I think the teacher said she's from Croatia. I'm not even sure where that is because we haven't yet looked at world maps much in social studies.

Anyway, she looks different, and she's pretty shy. She talks funny too, when she talks, but I think that's because she's still learning English. I see her kinda hang her head down in class when she's trying to do schoolwork. I think she has a hard time understanding everything.

Sometimes she wears funny clothes. Well, they're pretty nice, but they look like they come from another country or something, you know. Old-fashioned, I think my mommy would call it.

Well, my friends aren't very nice to her. And some other kids aren't either. They make fun of her behind her back, roll their eyes when she says something wrong in class, giggle when they walk past her in the hall, hold their nose when she eats her snack of something that smells like burned toast. So Adelina doesn't have any friends, except Cora Kort who's cross-eyed and has real ugly thick glasses, and she's real short and shows off all the time how dumb she is. I mean, nobody likes Cora, though teacher says we have to be nice to her. Well, my dad says you have to be nice to icky spiders too, but you don't have to like them, do you?

Anyway, I was thinking of Adelina. I think she's lonely and unhappy. I feel sort of sorry for her and get mad at my friends for treating her so bad. And then they get mad at me. So I wonder what to do. If I try to be nice to Adelina, then maybe Cora will expect me to be nice to her too, and I certainly don't want to give her the idea that I want to be her friend too. Besides, I'll be in trouble with my other friends. And I don't want to lose them. I just don't know what to do.

What would you do, Lord?

❦ TO PONDER ❦
What would *you* tell her?

Voices of Children and Youth

- Dear Lord, I can't get to sleep. I think I ate too many Oreos. My tummy hurts. Please make the hurt go away. I promise not to empty the jar again. And Lord, help Mommy not get too mad when she finds out.

- Thank you, Lord, for the "C" I got in science today. A "B" would've been nice, but you know that school is hard for me. I wish I was smart, like Freddy. I try lots harder than he does, and he gets "A's." Why can't we all be the same, Lord?

- Dear Jesus, help Mommy and Daddy not to fight so much. Can you please make the devil go away, so Mommy won't cry so much and Daddy will play with me again? Please?

- I don't know if I should pray about this, Lord. There's nothing in the Bible about dating. But I sure like that girl in my Religion class. She's probably not even noticed me. I'm not much to look at or anything and I'm pretty shy. But I think she's really cool. She's not so phony like a lot of them. I like what she has to say in discussions. I don't know, Lord, but it sure would be nice to get to know her better.

- I wanna sleep, Lord. I'm so tired. But my tummy is too empty. Make the hunger go away, Lord. And help my mama get some money for food tomorrow.

- Oh Lord, why can't I have lots of friends like everybody else? Why do so many kids I'd like to be friends with act snotty to me? It's so depressing. Sometimes I hate myself 'cause I don't seem good enough for anybody. I need friends, Lord.

- I'm scared in the dark, Lord, and my daddy won't let me turn the light on. Please don't let anything bad happen to me. Let me fall asleep quick so I won't have to see the dark anymore.

- I feel pretty rotten, Lord. I keep hearing the coach yelling at me in front of the whole team. It was just a mistake, Lord. Why did he have to get so mad and make me look like such a fool? I didn't even want to talk to anybody after that. And I don't feel like playing anymore. What am I going to do, Lord?

- Dear Lord, thank you for making my teddy all better. He can see real good with both eyes again now. Can you make Gramma's eyes better too? Then maybe she can read to me again.

- Lord, I'm sorry I cheated on my chem test today. I know lots of kids who cheat, but that doesn't make it right, I know. My conscience is bothering me now. It tells me that I should tell the teacher what I did. Maybe it's you telling me. But I'm scared, Lord. I don't think I can do it. I'm not sure I want to. Even though I know it's the right thing to do. But the teacher would hate me, and I'd probably flunk the course. I can't afford that. Can I, Lord? Are you going to hate me if I do nothing? Please help me, Lord.

- Lord, thank you for Mommy and Daddy and all my friends and the fun things I got to do on my birthday, and—thank you for Annie not telling on me when I stuck a popcorn in her ear. I won't do it again, Lord—I promise.

∽ TO PONDER ∽
Are you listening to *your* child?

LOVE

There's a children's story about two hares; it's a story about love:

Papa Hare and Little Hare are relaxing in the grass under a tree.
To the West, the sun is slowly descending from the sky.
Already the wispy clouds close to the horizon are tinting
    with pink.
It's that special time when a feeling comes that all is right with
    the world.

Little Hare snuggles closer to Papa Hare, his little snub nose
    buried in Papa's soft fur.
"I love you, Daddy," he whispers.
Suddenly he gets up, stands a bit unsteadily on his hind legs,
    spreads out his front legs like arms as wide as they will reach,
    and says: "That's how much I love you, Daddy."
Papa Hare looks up at his little boy, slowly gets up on his long
    hind legs, stretches his body at full length, and with much
    longer arms spread wide, says: "And that's how much I
    love you."
Hmm, that's quite a lot, thinks Little Hare.
"As high as I can reach, that's how much I love you," he says,
    and he raises his short arms toward the dusky sky.
"As high as I can reach, that's how much I love you," responds
    Papa Hare, and his arms almost reach the lowest branch of
    the tree.
That's pretty high, thinks Little Hare, I wish my arms were
    that long.
He looks through the branches up at the darkening sky and sees
    a slice of the moon.
"As far as the moon, that's how much I love you," he yawns, and
    closes his eyes.
"Oh, that is far," says Papa Hare. "That is very, very far," and
    gently lays Little Hare into his bed of leaves. He bends down

and kisses his son goodnight. Then he pulls close to Little
Hare and whispers with a smile, "As far as the moon—
AND BACK."

"I love you, Yahweh," said Noah, ignored the mockery of
neighbors and friends, built his ark, and saved what God had
made.

"I love you, Yahweh," said Abram, turned his back on comfort
and security for an uncertain, wandering future, and became
the father of believers.

"I love you, Yahweh," said Moses, embraced disgrace rather than
esteem, and led God's people out of slavery.

"I love you, Yahweh," said Daniel, defied the authority of the
king, and showed God's power to save inside the lions den.

"I love you, Lord," said Peter, forgiven for his betrayal, and
became a fearless fisher of men.

"I love you, Abba," said Jesus, took up his cross, and died for us.

"I love you, Father," has come through the ages from boys and
girls, men and women who have shown their love through
small and large deeds of courage, obedience, and faith.

May it always be so, with the Father tenderly bending over his
little children, breathing on us the words of power and of
peace: "As high as the heavens are above the earth, and as far
as the east is from the west, that's how much I love you."

Thank you, Abba.

A Prayer for the Children

We pray for the children
   who sneak popsicles before supper,
   who erase holes in math workbooks,
   who can never find their shoes.
And we pray for those
   who stare at photographers from behind barbed wire,
   who can't bound down the street in a new pair of sneakers,
   who never "counted potatoes,"
   who are born in places where we wouldn't be caught dead,
   who never go to the circus,
   who live in an X-rated world.
We pray for children
   who bring us sticky kisses and share jelly beans from
      grimy fists,
   who hug us in a hurry and forget their hot lunch money.
And we pray for those
   who never get dessert,
   who have no comfort blanket to drag behind them,
   who watch their parents watch them die,
   who can't find any bread to steal,
   who don't have any rooms to clean up,
   whose pictures aren't on anybody's dresser,
   whose monsters are real.
We pray for children
   who spend all their allowance before Tuesday,
   who throw tantrums in the grocery store and pick at
      their nose,
   who like ghost stories, who shove dirty clothes under
      their bed,
   who never rinse out their tub,
   who get visits from the tooth fairy,
   who don't like to be kissed in front of the carpool,
   who squirm in church and scream in the phone,
   whose tears we sometimes laugh at and
   whose smiles can make us cry.

And we pray for those
  whose nightmares come in the daytime,
  who will eat anything,
  who have never seen a dentist,
  who aren't spoiled by anybody,
  who go to bed hungry and cry themselves to sleep,
  who live and move but have no being.
We pray for children
  who want to be carried and for those who must,
  for those who don't get a second chance,
  for those we smother and …
  for those who will grab the hand of anybody kind enough to
    offer it.

Dear Lord, come to your children when they can't come to you.

—adapted from a poem by "Anonymous,"
in memory of the children and teacher killed on March 24, 1998, in Jonesboro, AR

Teenagers

Do you love them, Lord?

Yes, I know, you love all your children.
But really now, don't they get on your nerves sometimes?
Don't they wear your patience thin like a frazzled fiber,
ready to snap?

You know what I mean, Lord.
Their tongues, I mean:
sweeter than a honeycomb one minute,
dripping acid the next.

Their feelings, I mean:
HANDLE WITH CARE
written all over them,
so sensitive...
and often tenderhearted
affectionate
loving;
but then those awful mood swings to
tough
cold
and hurtful.

Their behavior, I mean:
one day a model of Christian kindness
thoughtfulness
and helpfulness;
the next, a monster who struts and frets
who rants and raves
as if struck by a sudden personality mutation.

Their needs, I mean:
so dependent on the

interest
encouragement
and love of parents;
but equally in need of
"space"
freedom of choice
exercise of independence.

Am I right, Lord?

Your description sounds familiar to me.
In fact, it seems to fit you to a tee.

Ouch!
I'm embarrassed.
Confession time.
Yes, in too many ways I am your spiritual teenager,
confused and contradictory
reaching so eagerly for maturity in Christ
but too often distracted by pressures and problems.

Forgive me, Lord.
And please be patient with me.

I love you.
Let that work through your mind
into your heart.
But I love teenagers especially.
My image still shines brightly in them.
They're so eager to grow.
They feel deeply.
They're impatient with the wrongs all around them.
They're quick to spot hypocrisy.
They do not pretend.
They have strong ideals.
They look for truth
and are eager to follow it.

They look for faith
and are eager to embrace it.
They look for love
and are eager to give it.
Yes, teenagers are dear to my heart.

Thank you for teaching me again, Lord.
You know that I love them too.
They too are fearfully and wonderfully made:
minds expanding
hormones flowing
faith unfolding.
Keep us from getting in the way
of their growing:
wise to know when to stand aside
and when to lend a helping hand
and give an encouraging word.

Use us, we pray:
to model a thoughtful
caring
Christ-filled life;
to practice what we preach;
to add fun and zest and joy
to their young lives;
to give direction and correction;
to leave a legacy of love
for them
for others
for You—
with your Spirit's help.

⌒ TO PONDER ⌒
What does *your* teenager need most from you?

About Graduates

They make parents proud, Lord—proud to watch their kids climbing the rungs of the educational ladder from the first awkward struggles with letters and sounds to the writing of a 30-page seminar paper on the aesthetic and spiritual tension in the life and selected works of John Donne. And we're proud to see them reach a landing for a good long breather now and again.

But they make us mostly grateful, Lord:

> for your gifts of knowledge and understanding;
> for your gifts of good teachers who make learning an adventure;
> for your gifts of inquiry and reflection that help shape the growing soul.

You know, Lord, that classroom learning is neither easy nor palatable for everyone. You haven't made everyone the same, and we trust you have your reasons. At a time when many of the young give themselves to drugs and crime and cynicism, we are grateful for every graduate who struggled honorably and succeeded; though the name never made the school's honor roll, we know it is on yours and therefore on ours.

We pray for all of them, Lord. Help them to pass on to others the good they have received. May they be eager to receive from others what will enrich and bless them. Help them to discover that loving, enjoying, caring, and understanding are forces in life more powerful than getting and winning and spending. Help them to stay in touch with the joys and heartaches of self and others and thereby nurture their humanity.

May they never crave the opinion and approval of the crowd whose standards vary and whose praise is fickle. Help them to stand on their own two feet in the way of truth and justice. May they not fear ambiguity or complexity. May they not be afraid of making mistakes. May they not bow to pressure to compromise principle or integrity or faith.

Help them to engage the world as it is while they work unceasingly to make it what you meant it to be. Save them from the fears that lead to fanaticism, to suspicion and rejection of others. Show them the good that must be embraced and celebrated in your name.

Listen to them when they wonder what life holds for them, what to do with their education, what you expect of them, whom they should marry, where they should live. You have promised to guide and direct, and that's a comfort.

Bless them with good friends, Lord; with strong faith; with contentment.

Thank you for our graduates, Lord. Your world has much need of them. We commend them to your care and keeping.

THEN THERE WAS ONE

First there was one.

She came a bit sooner than our pre-marital plans had projected. Three or four years, we had thought, reasonably. That would give us time to sit across the table from each other and learn the fine art of dinner conversation, enjoy each other's company, adjust to each other's quirks and quips, but also to get some more education and even put a few bucks in the bank. Maybe. D.V.

But she—our first one—wasn't to be put off that long. Less than two years into our marriage, and a roly-poly babe came between us—and brought us closer still. She looked like baby Winston, but acted like the WWII Churchill: very much in charge. But she was ours, and we were proud.

We thought she would be our one and only for a while. Maybe for quite a while. There were still those other plans. But, somehow, family planning wasn't one of them, or so it seemed. Another surprise package was delivered before number one had successfully completed her Potty Training Course.

Then there were two.

Nice size family, we reasoned. Or rationalized. And number two was so cuddly and so content to follow the burgeoning leadership of her older sister. More education would just have to wait a bit, and the bank would have to give us some money now, but little kids are nice and such a blessing, right? They were, too.

But as snowflakes often turn into a squall, and a few raindrops into a shower, so a couple of kids can turn into a population explosion. Or so it seemed when a busy baby-bathing-burping-bouncing year later, a little junior joined the Baron Brood.

And now there were three.

Three is of course a fine number. It's also a crowd. And we had to find and make room for it in our modestly-sized home. Not so simple, really, for a house is not as expandable as a heart. And our hearts gave us no trouble; it proved easy to open them to the uniqueness of each one, to be filled with those fearfully made little family members with an intensity and possessiveness that is familiar to all parental love. As for the house—we moved into a larger one.

And then there were four.

Now our house was full: of bibs and baby beds, of toys and teething rings, of cooing and crying, of diapers and dada talk. I think the children sort of raised each other through those early years. Number one of course would lead; fun-loving number two would follow; gentle-smiling number three would contribute peace; and crayon-wielding number four would decorate—everything. No one would complain of loneliness or boredom. Those were busy moonlighting, diaper-folding, smock-wearing years, but they were good years. There were few luxuries, but our house and life were full. And we were content.

But there came the day—not long thereafter, for family time is never long—when we found ourselves saying goodbye to our number one who, for reasons more easily understood by the head than accepted by the heart, had just married and was now moving 1500 miles away. In those years when children grow from infancy to young adulthood, parents learn some difficult lessons: of giving and forgiving, of tolerance and toughness, of speaking and keeping still. But as we watched the car of the newlyweds drive away, we had to learn the new and more painful lesson of letting go.

Number one had left.

In less than six years of married life, our brood of four had come to fill the nest. And since they seemed to have come sort of all at once, it was only logical to expect their leaving to be the same. Predictable and logical. Except that love is not logical and hardly reasonable. Love does not expect anyone to go, at least not far away, and never permanently. When a young adult, I thought it silly of people who were reluctant to let their offspring move to far-away places. Now as a parent, I thought it eminently defensible and natural to want children within easy driving distance.

True, there had been a time when we wished for some peace and quiet. But then came the time when we would welcome the slap of the screen door and familiar voices shout their greetings. There had been a time when we could reach across the table and touch each one. Then came the time when we had to call long distance. The house became larger again; bedrooms stood empty. Maybe our hearts shrunk a little too.

But the nest did not empty out completely. And the house did not fall silent.

Though four left, there was still one. And the Special Care package that arrived, surprise-surprise, so many years later, did her best to equal the verve and energy of all four older siblings. She nearly managed. There would come the day when she too would leave. But for a goodly number of years she was very much with us, and we were grateful for that blessing.

And though the others flew far away, they did return now and again. (They had much to come back for, after all. Though they left bedrooms empty, the basement was full of their boxes. Maybe children never quite leave home. My mother 2500 miles away stored boxes of my childhood treasures till she was into her 90s.) But whatever brings them back when they come, our arms are always open, and our embraces tight, as we whisper: "Welcome home...we missed you...we love you." Those are always special, heart-filling times, for you discover that when your children leave, they become more precious still.

And that makes me wonder now. When at last we as children return to our heavenly home, will you, our Father, stand at the door too, with arms stretched wide? Will we feel your embrace and hear you whisper: "Welcome home...I missed you...I love you"?

Then our hearts will overflow and our joy will be complete.

☙ TO PONDER ❧
...and then there are children who have no home...

Parents and Children

You're 35 years old, or 40, or 45, but there you are, crawling on all fours and barking like a dog while your little toddler howls hysterically and tries to hoist herself up onto the back of the barking monster. Or you're pulling an eager three-year old onto your lap, her favorite blankie wrapped around, comfortably settling in for another episode from the exciting saga of make-believe Ratfink or for a tenth re-reading of "Jack and the Beanstalk." Or you're out on the driveway, modeling the perfect lay-up for your future star basketball player. For the moment you're a child again. And that's why parents need children—to remember their own early years, to remember who they were and what they did before they grew up, to revive and perpetuate the playfulness and imagination and fantasies of childhood days that were magic then and are magic still.

You're late for church, so you're pushing the pedal to the metal; after all, it won't do to come after the introit for the fourth Sunday in a row. But little eagle eyes in the back seat hardly needs a megaphone: "You're going ten miles over the speed limit, Daddy!" It's as effective as any siren.

Or you're sitting around the dinner table, just after Bible reading, when some perversity entices you into a heated argument with your wife over the consequential issue whether boiling water should steep for two or three minutes before pouring over the Lipton teabag. Out of the corner of your eye you catch the confused look on junior's face, and at once you remember the words just read: "Does anyone think of himself as a religious man? If he does not control his tongue, his religion is worthless and he deceives himself."

Children are acute observers: they spot your slightest defect and inconsistency a mile away. That's why parents need children; to see ourselves through the eyes of our children is to squirm uncomfortably and guiltily sometimes, but it is also a stern and much-needed corrective—for our growth as Christians and for our modeling as parents. Our children learn, after all, most from their observations of the actions, words, tone, and looks of those with whom they live.

You're in your teenager's bedroom. You suspect her of drug use, of hanging out with the wrong crowd, of going to the wrong parties, of compromising or even losing her faith. But your probing and pleading meet only sullen silence.

Or you're sitting by the hospital bed of your oldest: you know from the medical reports that you're in danger of losing him. You hold his young hand in your own, and you want desperately to never let it go.

That's when you learn to pray. Children can bend the straightest knees and humble the proudest hearts. They can teach us in painful ways our absolute need of you, oh God, and make us discover, even and maybe especially through tears, the grace that comes from our adoption by you, our Father.

You are old now and living alone with many other aged in one large building. The care is good and the companions are nice, but they're not the friends of your youth or of your adult life; those are mostly gone now, as is your life's partner. What gives you most delight still are the visits of your children—their cheerfulness, their touches of thoughtfulness, their presence and all the memories they embody of years that slipped by so quickly but still are relived in the mind on many a long evening when the shadows push the present back into the past.

Or you're bedridden now and gradually learning the last lesson: to let go of life. Doctors and nurses come and go; some people from your church too. But what matters most in these waning hours of life is the presence of your children. They hold your hand now, they feed you and read to you and pray for you, and sometimes they sit in silence, but they're there, and you relish their nearness, especially on this last journey. That journey is easier in the company of your children, in the presence of their care and concern. They've always been part of you as you've been part of them, and they sustain you now with the strength of their love.

Do children need parents? Of course they do. But parents need children too.

Thank you, Father, for our children.

~ TO PONDER ~
Do your children know how much you appreciate them?

LETTING GO

I saw them at an airport, parting from each other:
aged parents from their daughter and her little ones.
He, bent, feeble, eyes in distant stare
with no expression, as if detached already from what had
     been life.
She, hovering close, a help meet still, "until death ...."
much like a Picasso blue-period scene.
Quick hugs, no tears, their faces set toward flying home.
No backward glance, no final wave at dear ones left behind.
Their journey lay ahead, and there's no turning back from that.
The daughter, crying now, watching them go, and disappear,
not ready to let go what won't keep.

It's not an easy thing to learn, though we do not lack
     for practice;
to let go of mother's lap, her hand, her apron strings,
then enter the first strange world of school, of work, of life.
Or let go of innocence when evil shows its ugly face
where there was only good before.
Letting go of dreams that die when proven vain by chance
     or circumstance,
of relationships that break like teacups falling from the shelf.
Not easy as we let go of springtime flowers and summer skies,
watch fall colors fade, then float down to the earth,
soon covered under snow, like a white sheet drawn quickly
     over death.

Practice does not make perfect: it always hurts
to let good things go we counted on and needed in our life.
It's harder still to let go of ourselves, the self we love and hate,
the rags of self-indulgence, pride and greed,
and other sins that fester deep within our souls.

Help us, dear God, to let go what and when we must.
Grant us the grace to let go of youth and middle age

when the years take us to that point and past.
And when strength fades and impairments mount,
when loved ones fly away and we try to cling
to what we cannot hold and keep,
and when at last our own health fails and we take our
    final breath—
hold us securely in your hand, dear Lord of life and death,
through the cold shadows and the dark of night,
and lead us into everlasting light.

FORGIVENESS, GRACE, AND HOPE

*The Christian faith journey often follows some
unexpected paths.*

*Sometimes a path can lead to life-changing
encounters.*

An encounter with the mystery of forgiveness.

*An encounter with human and divine goodness
and grace that sweetens the soul.*

*An encounter with danger and terror that buckle
the knees into prayer.*

*An encounter with Christ as your Savior that
transforms belief into faith.*

*An encounter with Hope as essential to the
Christian's journey.*

WHO IS JESUS?
JOHN 7 & 8

Ever since you came among us, Lord, people have asked the
    question, "Who is Jesus?"
We have too.
No question is more important. Our life depends on it.
We've been listening to some answers, Lord. We find ourselves
    among the questioning crowd surrounding you on the
    temple square,
and we hear you say forthrightly: "I am the light of the world!"

The words of Isaiah echo in our head:
"The people who walked in darkness have seen a great light!"
Again we hear the voice by the temple exclaim:
"Let those who thirst come to me and let them drink!"

We know that without light and water there can be no life.
And, in fact, we've seen that those who walk with you
are in the light; and we believe that those who drink from the
    living water shall never thirst again.

But we see the scorn on people's faces,
We see them pick up stones to close the well, to smash the light,
to doom themselves to wander in the darkness,
lost in an endless, arid desert, where they will surely die.

Did it grieve you, Lord, to see murder in their eyes instead
    of faith?
Does it grieve you when we also turn our back on the source
    of light,
stumble and fall in the darkness of our own making,
and blindly curse our plight?

Now, because your time had not yet come, you slip away from
    temple square, from those who did not know you, Lord,

from those who scream their unbelief and hate—
when your eye falls on the blind man sitting in the gate,
who's never seen the light.
In that one man you see the grief of the whole world,
and the blindness of us all.
Full of compassion, you stop to give him sight,
for that's who Jesus is.

Dear Lord, when we forget to walk with you,
then heal our blindness too.

TO PONDER

Who is Jesus in *your* life?

FORGIVENESS

It hit me like it never had before.
Those words, just before the elements:
"...remember and believe that the precious blood of our Lord
　　Jesus Christ
was shed for the complete forgiveness of all our sins."
The complete forgiveness of all my sins?
My God, I don't think I've ever really believed that.
In my head I have, of course.
It's part of the doctrine I learned a long time ago: "Our Lord
　　Jesus Christ was given us to set us completely free and to
　　make us right with God."
But in my heart? I don't think so.

—why not?—

That's what I'm trying to figure out.

—because it's too easy?—

Yeah, maybe that's it.

—it wasn't for Him, though—

I know, and that's the problem. Why should Jesus do all that for
　　me! I don't deserve it.

—because I love you—

And every time I hear that, the tears come.
Because I'm not that lovable.
I've done nothing to be worthy of it.
And then I think it can't be true.
I can see a man sacrificing his life for God—but God sacrificing
　　his life for a man?

And if he did, if he really did—I owe him big time!
I've got to spend my whole life trying to prove to him that his
    death was not in vain, trying to show gratitude for what he
    did for me.

—and that burden of obligation weighs heavily on you—

Yes, yes, it does.
Instead of grateful I feel guilty, because I keep screwing up.

—how so?—

I'm never as consistently loving and giving and honorable and
    dedicated as I should be.

—so you think I must be disappointed?—

Yes, because I keep letting you down!

—yes, you do, but that's not why—

What do you mean?

*—you let me down, because you won't accept what I'm trying to give
    you—*

What's that?

—my love; my complete forgiveness of all your sins—

—you're silent—

It's those tears again.
Because it's so beautiful, and so amazing.
Oh God, I want it and need it so much.

But is it really true? Is it really possible?
—*oh you of little faith*—

Yes, that's it exactly.
My faith is too small to embrace that much grace.
I'm sorry. What do I do?

—*he who comes to me will never go hungry; he who believes in me will
    never be thirsty*—

Oh Father, keep me coming, for I want to believe; will you help
    me in my unbelief?
And God, thank you for that unspeakable gift of your son
    Jesus Christ.

—*let that gift, through the Holy Spirit, change your life, my child, now
    and forevermore*—

Amen. Amen.

TO PONDER
Why do we feel we must be deserving of forgiveness?

OF MOMENTS AND MEMORY

What is time but a myriad of moments merging in one constant flux of changing sensations, impressions, fragments of thoughts, and words. In retrospect we hardly distinguish one moment, one fragment from another.

Yet all our past moments follow us. A few even manage to stand out clearly and distinctly in our memory. It is such especially that give character and force and meaning to our present moments; it is such especially that constitute the life of the soul. Such moments become sacred to us, because in passing through us they took part of ourselves or left with us a part of another.

The sounds of roaring planes and angry guns awakened me one night. Scared, I tried to hide more deeply under the blankets, at the same time crawling closer to my older brother. But soon Dad came through the darkness in the room and quietly told us to get dressed and come to the kitchen.

We groped for our clothes in the dark. It was wartime in Holland, and any show of light was strictly forbidden. We dressed hastily and gathered in the kitchen then, a single candle playing grotesquely with our shadows against the walls and ceiling, while in the air above us others fought against the shadow of death.

We huddled together, silent and scared.

Then came the moment that for me hallowed that place and time forever in my memory.

Dad asked us to kneel.

We had never knelt in prayer before as a family.

But we knelt that night in the flickering shadows, and Dad prayed for us, his voice pleading above the din of war for protection, for peace, for faith and trust.

We went outside after that and watched planes fighting and falling, parachutes drifting in the light of the firebombs exploding all around. It was a fearful spectacle, and yet to me, then and now, not nearly as impressive or memorable as that sacred moment when our knees touched the cold linoleum of the kitchen floor in prayer that reached out to the mystery and power of God.

Slightly more than a decade later, on an early morning in November, I was startled out of sleep, not now by screaming aircraft or wailing sirens but by the moaning of a man in mortal agony.

Something was seriously wrong with Dad.

He must have known it too.

For between the violent pains that wracked his body and made him scream in anguish, he asked his children who were home to come to his bed, alone.

What I remember most vividly from those few private moments with my dad was his embrace, his kiss, and his final question:

"Will you forgive me for all I've done against you?"

I was stunned.

A wave of emotion swept through me. Its force affects me still.

Whatever remnants of resentment a son's heart might still have harbored against his father vanished forever in that moment.

I knew that I too had need to ask his forgiveness.

But I could not speak; I could only nod and clasp his hand and kiss his cheek.

Time fades many moments of the past.

But thank you, God, that there are some that glow more brightly as moments turn into years and decades, moments so full of grace and import that our lives would be strangely void without them.

Each of us has had such moments.

They bless our lives as we recall, express, and give thanks for them.

For they make your mystery, your power, and your love, oh God, more palpable.

Thank you, Lord.

~ TO PONDER ~

What "holy moments" have blessed *your* life?

GRACE

We had just walked the distance from the American Consulate
to the central station in the heart of Munich. It was Friday
evening rush hour; hundreds of commuters were scurrying in
every direction to waiting buses and trains. We stood there, the
two of us, in the midst of that frantic bustle, wondering how we
would ever find our way through it and out of it, into Austria,
where we hoped to catch up with the other tour members.

As one of two chaperones of a group of high school students,
I had stayed behind in Munich with a young man who had lost
his passport. We had spent most of the day at the police station
and the American Consulate. At last my companion had received
a new passport; then we had hurried to central station in hopes
of catching a train or bus that would reunite us with our group.

We stood there, bewildered, staring at the dozens of buses and
trains that seemed to be coming and going every few seconds. It
wasn't the language barrier that was so bewildering. As a former
German teacher, I had had much practice that week in stuttering
guttural utterings. No, it was rather the sense of lostness, not
unfamiliar to a pre-schooler on her first day of school, standing
on the playground, for the moment cut off from her own kind,
and sensing all around her the rushing bodies of big third and
fourth graders who know exactly where they are going.

That is how we felt. But then out of nowhere an American-
sounding voice cut through with "Watcha doing, watching all
the girls go by?"

As it turned out, the voice belonged to a thirty-ish German
gentleman on his way home from the airport where he was
employed. As a German civilian, he had worked with the U.S.
Army Signal Corps, hence his eagerness to practice his American
idioms on a couple of forlorn-looking tourists.

He spent the next three or four hours with us, checking
into schedules, calling the Austrian hotel where our group was
staying, directing us to the right ticket booth for the first bus
out the next morning, arranging for our night's lodging in a

nearby hotel, and dining with us leisurely, surrounded by the "gemütlichkeit" of a German pub.

I have vivid memories of another incident, this one more recent. It was raining hard when I drove up the steep hill toward Simon Fraser University in British Columbia. It was my first visit and it took me awhile to find the visitor's parking lot. When I was going to drive in, I discovered a gate barring the way, the kind that requires money for it to raise. I dashed out through cascading Northwest rain to find out what kind of coins was needed. Students on the way to class were rushing by, eager to reach dry ground. All except one. One young woman student noticed my ignorance and stopped to inform me that it would take exactly two Canadian quarters to admit my car to the lot. But I had no quarters, Canadian or American. And the rain fell harder. I asked her if she had change for a dollar. It was a stupid question; how many students carry four quarters on them. And fewer still would stop in the rain to look for them. But, soaked by now, she fished in her purse, found two quarters, and dropped them in the slot for me. The bar swung up as I, taken by surprise again, offered the gracious young lady my American dollar. She shook her head with a wet smile, wished me a nice day, and hurried after her friends.

There have been other such occasions; and most people, I hope, can tell similar and more dramatic stories. But for me that does not diminish their surprise or beauty. In fact, I feel awe-struck that anyone should freely give of self for the sake of a stranger. The man in Bavaria and the woman in B.C. did not know me and owed me nothing. They gave me what I had not deserved, and they gave it freely, with no strings attached. Such giving never fails to surprise by joy.

Father, help us remember and celebrate the kindness of others and give them thanks. Help us take time to reach out in kindness to others, even the stranger, who need our help. And Father, we want to especially stammer out our gratitude to you, our God, who in his amazing grace reached out to us, undeserving and estranged and even hostile, and freely gave us the dearest gift he could, the Son, so that even if we should have little else, we would yet have everything.

Let that grace fill us with awe, with dumbfounded thankfulness, and with the Spirit's impulse to extend such self-giving in the Father's name to others.

> ⚘ TO PONDER ⚘
>
> **Recall an instance of grace-receiving and giving in *your* life.**

CONFESSION

I'm angry, Lord.
Cancer is touching one after another,
sneering like a concentration camp guard who has victims tagged.
Who will be next to get the nod?
Who created this monster that invisibly invades
vital parts of our body to begin its deadly work?
Is it we, oh Lord?
Surely no malignant cells issue from the Creator's hand?
What have we done to our world, which belongs to you, to
     spawn this scourge?
What have we done to our body, which belongs to you, to feed
     this predator?
I'm angry, because we have failed.
We have failed to be good earth-keepers.
We are selfish and pollute the air we breathe.
We make products that fill our coffers, but our coffins too.
We are self-indulgent and harm our health.
We smoke and eat and drink and work ourselves to death.
I'm angry, for people I love have died, are dying, because
     we failed
to insure the safety of food and air,
or failed to provide the necessary information.
I'm angry, for some have died, are dying, because they failed
to care for their own body as God's temple,
to treat it with the love and care with which God made it.

How can we explain, excuse, or defend the callous disrespect
with which we treat that which God made so good?
The wanton ways in which we poison the environment God gave
     for our delight?
The blindness or weakness by which we indulge appetites
     and desires
cravings and addictions that destroy vital organs
which God gave for our life and his service?

I'm angry, Lord, angry at how we have failed you, each other, and
    ourselves.

Oh Lord, have mercy.
Oh Lord, forgive.
Oh Lord, help us to change.
Oh Lord, help us to practice what you teach us.
For your Kingdom.
By your power.
To your glory.

SEPTEMBER 11, 2001:
A CONTEMPORARY TESTIMONY

Oh God of heaven and earth,
in the face of great evil that wracks with rage and fear,
out of the rubble of smashed buildings and shattered lives,
we rise as your people, and through our tears
we proclaim, around the world you loved enough to die for,
to those who hate the world enough to kill for:
that our world belongs to God!

In that world we renounce the works of darkness
that in the twisted fervor of religious zealotry,
in the name of Allah or ego or power or hate,
are bent on destroying all that defies their will and ways.

Yes, there is much we do not understand,
how in horrific tragedy, you, God Almighty,
have all things under your control,
and in divine providence direct all things to their end,
but we have known the balm of your amazing grace,
and believe that you hold this whole world in your hand.

We confess that sin is present everywhere:
in the pride of religion or race,
in the arrogance of nations, in the worship of false gods.
We repent, oh God, for all the self-serving ways
in which we fail to show your face.

Oh God, have mercy and forgive.
Have mercy on a scarred and broken world,
stand by us in our need, show us your care,
heal our hurts, hold us when fears shake us, keep us from strife.
Move us each day anew to faith and trust,
to do your kingdom work on this needy earth,

to be the community of compassion for all who suffer,
to walk humbly with our God, love mercy, and do what's just.

We pray for rulers, Lord.
Use us to help governments know your will for public life,
to stop killings and make violence cease,
to ensure the dignity and welfare of all,
to promote order and harmony,
to act in wisdom and seek peace.

For this world belongs to God divine.
To it you turn your face in love.
And we, your people, hold fast to your word,
that evil shall not overcome the good,
that light piercing the darkness from above
shall never cease to shine.

Shine, Jesus, shine!

FROM WITNESS TO WORSHIP

When I first heard about him, I was puzzled at his obscure birth in Bethlehem, stashed away in a smelly stall where only some simple, incoherent shepherds rushed in to look at this little lamb of God.

I was more impressed when later some more sophisticated scientists from the East came to the city slums to bring their worship, and their fancy presents too.

But when some years later I heard him in the temple, asking questions I could hardly understand, I knew that this was no ordinary child. Those learned doctors of theology were dumbfounded too. I couldn't help but glow with vicarious pride, as if he were my kid brother, a wunderkind, and not even a teenager yet! I vowed to keep an eye on him, for I knew he would be famous.

He wasn't, at least not for a long time. But at that wedding in Cana, I knew he was on the way at last. This man had power, that was obvious. And I liked his unassuming way of using it.

Except when he got angry. I felt like clapping and cheering all the way through his rampage of the temple money market when he put the fear of God into those courtyard capitalists, those pigeon peddlers who preferred profits to prayers. I felt the same way when he called those phony Pharisees hypocrites and vipers and blind fools, right to their faces. No one had ever had the gall to do that, though many had wanted to. He got away with it too. No, there was no denying the power of his authority. And when he exercised it, it was awe-some.

Like the time on that stormy Sea of Galilee. Irritated because his fearful friends interrupted a much-needed nap, he shouted at the glowering clouds and leaping waves to behave themselves; and they did. His friends nearly fell overboard, more afraid of his power now than they had been of the storm.

I admired him not only when he showed his mettle. Maybe I admired him even more when he used this special power to make others feel better. I wanted to shout and dance through that multitude of munchers when he put on the biggest instant all-you-can-eat picnic you ever saw, with nothing more than a few loaves and a couple fish, and all because he didn't want them to go home on an empty stomach.

And I wanted to cry with the widow when she clung to her son and the gift of his dear, new life. There were so many such times when I felt myself glorying in him as he used his special power and authority to raise the helpless and the humble and to humble the haughty spirit and the scheming mind.

He had his enemies, of course; a good man always does. But I didn't worry about him. I had seen him more than once walk unscathed through crowds with murder on their minds. He was my hero, a hero I thought would live forever.

When I stood by his cross, therefore, just outside the unholy city on that Friday afternoon, and watched him dying like a common criminal right before my disbelieving eyes, I felt the devastation of betrayal. Where was now his power and authority? Why had he suffered so passively the lies, the ridicule, the flogging, the screams of blood-thirsty crowds? And why was he dying now, not even like a martyr, but merely as a substitute for an outlaw called Barabbas? What had been the point of such a life, and what was the point of such a death? Where was this God whom he had claimed as Father? Maybe as fickle as his friends, forsaking him when most needed? What kind of God was that, or was there none?

The sudden darkness of the afternoon descended on my soul, and I fled from Golgotha. I wanted no more heroes, no more illusions of superhuman power and authority and goodness. I would simply settle for whatever could make sense to a mind skeptical of all things untypical, unscientific, unexplainable.

But it wouldn't be that simple. I discovered that a few days later. Everybody was talking about it. I felt annoyed at this new disturbance of my yet unsettled peace. I wanted to shout that it was not so, that it could not be, that a dead man does not rise again. For I was trying to make my peace with the death of my dreams, and I wasn't ready to resurrect them—not yet, not really at all.

Still, I believed the story, incredible as it was. I believed it,
for I had seen him raise the widow's son. I believed it, for I
had always wanted to, from that first day that I had felt that
extraordinary presence within him and around him. Yes, I
believed it, though I never saw the risen Christ.

But my belief was in an idea, not a person. True, it was
a grandiose idea of a supernatural domain, but from which
I felt personally excluded. Hence, my belief did not nourish
me nor fulfill my growing need to feel a part of that awesome
power that could lay down life and take it up again. Nor did
my belief enlighten me about the meaning of that confusing,
painful Passion Week. For until now, I had met my hero, but
not my Savior. I had witnessed a wonder worker, but I had
not worshipped a servant-king. I had admired the stature of a
superman, but I had not loved him as my brother. I had belief,
but I had no faith.

That would come later, slowly, tentatively, sometimes in
breathless anticipation, but then again constrained by rational
remonstrations that would almost shut the spirit from the heart.
Actually, I'm still learning, growing now. I'm still learning to live
into and out of the feeling that I was worth dying for, that I am
loved with an undying love. It seems so much more reasonable
that a subject should die for his king instead. But I am growing
in the grace that allows a son to accept his Father's love and
a Brother's sacrifice. Often, as now, that grace is enough to
"dissolve my heart in thankfulness, and melt mine eyes to tears."

➣ TO PONDER ➣
Is there a difference between belief and faith?

NUMBER ONE

Yes, maybe every eel wants to become a whale.
It's fallen human nature to look out for number one.
Hence we need no help with winning but with losing.
We need training in submission of the will.
Submission to your voice, Lord, we so often slight:
"No one should be looking out for self,
but for the interest of others."
You tell us that we must be last, not first.
That we must not seek to rule, but serve.
That we seek not might and power,
but find ourselves among the meek.
That we do not cut off the hand that smites our cheek,
nor turn our back on those who're hard to love,
or seem less important than ourselves.
Also help us to submit, dear Lord,
to what is and cannot change,
to sickness, loss, and limitations,
not as defeated, struck with futility,
but learning that without submission,
there's a barrier between the self and God.
For we find no peace till we can say:
"Your will be done; sufficient is your grace."
Then the vaunted sovereignty of number one
yields to him who is the life, the truth, the way.

TO PONDER

What's #1 in *your* life?

WAITING

I've never been big on waiting, Lord.
But I remember waiting, even as a child:
the eager kind of waiting for my cousin to come home from
    school to play with me
for Sinterklaas to fill my stockings with toys and sweets
for ice to get thick enough to skate;
the anxious kind of waiting during the night for a knock on the
    windows from the Nazis
for the Canadian tanks to reach our town and liberate
for the end of Hitler and his reign of terror;
later, for a chance at education when doors were banging shut
for the end of a long hospital stay
for children to come home safely late in the night
for the report on emergency exploratory surgery of my spouse
for the world to change.

We're not very good at waiting, Lord.
We become impatient, tense, or fearful.
What we want, we want now.
If we can't have it, we become resentful, even bitter.

So remind us, Lord: waiting is part of our condition.
Abraham and Sarah waited for decades, till they gave up.
No doubt, Zechariah and Elizabeth did too.
How many years did Simeon and Anna wait to see salvation?
And how long has the Church waited for your Second Coming!

But be gracious, Father, to all who wait.
We know some who've waited long for friends,
for love, for spouse, and family;
for a child who's wandered far, to seek your face,
to come home, to be reconciled;
for healing from broken relationships,
the burden of depression, the ravages of disease;

and in many places, for food and work and what is just.
All of us are waiting for wars to cease,
for freedom to ring, for races to embrace.
Be gracious, Lord, for waiting is so hard
on faith and hope and trust.

Father, when there's nothing left to do for us but wait,
help us to shift our waiting to waiting for the Lord,
to yield what our hands clutched with desperation
to him who has the whole world in his hands.
Then we will truly join the whole creation,
waiting in eager anticipation
to see what God will do
in his good time, not ours.

Yes, Lord, by your grace help us accept our human limitation,
help us to listen and wait according to your Word:
"Be strong, take heart, and wait for the Lord."

➤ TO PONDER ➤
What are *you* waiting for?

ANTICIPATION

Many events are twice-experienced: first in our imagination, then reality.

And Shakespeare was right: "All things that are, are with more spirit chased than enjoyed."

Take a cross-country trip, for example, before the DVD revolution.

Months in advance, the anticipation begins to build as parents pore over maps and children excitedly chatter about whether or not Ahab and Jezebel, Mr. and Mrs. Gerbil, should share in the joys of the family trek. With the best-laid schemes eventually in place, the rubber at last hits the road. Before very long, the glamour and glory anticipated turns into monotonous, endless stretches of sterile interstates, the backseat becomes too small, and Twenty Questions played for the twentieth time becomes unbearably tiresome for all but the five-year old. Oh, there are high moments, of course, but they are invariably the unanticipated ones, like the dazzling display of aurora borealis one glittering camping night in a northern province, or the hike past cascading waterfalls to a mountain vista that literally takes your breath away.

In our anticipation we tend to glorify the ordinary or dream of the extraordinary. Our expectations are often sweeter than actual experience. Hence, disappointment.

But there are exceptions. Take the anticipation of a new birth. Weeks or months in advance, a new room is readied, the layette arranged, possible names reviewed. Brothers and sisters plan a decorated welcome-home party while parents imagine the tender joys of embracing new life. And then comes the trembling, fearful ecstasy of experiencing, and witnessing, the moment of birth, the moment when the dream becomes flesh, when that first cry announces the arrival of a unique addition to the human community. No anticipation can exceed or equal that moment. No imagination can fully anticipate the awesome wonder and heart-leaping joy of that event.

Father, you know that to live with anticipation is necessary. Anticipation nourishes hope, and life without hope will not endure. But no life can be free from disappointments. We dream of many things; we are blessed if we receive only half. And even those things we get, we have but for a season. It's what we never had that finally remains—in our anticipations, our hopes, our prayers, our faith. And when in your good time, Father, that faith vision is at last made real, when the last, cosmic journey reaches its final destiny, when the old, mortal life yields to the new, eternal—then, ah then... . But no human tongue or pen can tell us now. Until we see face to face, the anticipation is all we have. And on that anticipation rests the constancy of our faith.

GOING OUT INTO THE WORLD

*Children learn at too early an age that their world
   is a dangerous place.*
But there is much beauty too.
There are war makers and peacekeepers.
There are demons and angels.
*There are those whose desperate cries for help reach
   those who respond.*
There is much to lament and much to celebrate.
*And everywhere there is the call for those of faith to
   hear and to heal,*
to serve and to savor.

AFTER AFRICA

Lord, I thought I knew about Apartheid, but maybe it was
more the way Alaskans know about tornadoes.
I hadn't seen the consequences; I hadn't felt it in my guts.
Now I've walked the dirt path that meanders among the shacks,
the ramshackle shelters for blacks that skirt the cities of
    South Africa,
the human garbage dumps known as the "townships,"
the monstrous legacy of men of faith who on Sundays
prayed the Lord's Prayer, but decreed dehumanizing
people whose offense lay in the color of their skin.
Once they knew the dignity of homes, streets, and
    neighborhoods,
till bulldozers came and turned it all to rubble,
a barren wasteland as a monument to human cruelty.
Some have written of their tears, their anger, and their pain
in poignant language and a faith that I will not forget.
Dear Lord, restore the lives of those who have survived.

Lord, I heard of hunger, poverty, and the scourge of AIDS
    in Africa.
But now I've seen the dusty, arid places where almost
    nothing grows.
I've heard the weary, desperate tales from those who
    were attacked
by hostile tribes that stole their goats and burned their homes.
I've seen the haunted look in children's eyes, begging
for water, with tell-tale signs of malnutrition.
I've seen the children play in dirt, too poor to go to school.
Parents, too poor to seek a medic's care for a sick child,
or else a many hours walk from the nearest help.
I've seen too many orphans, whose parents died of AIDS,
and who themselves may well be facing the same fate.
Dear Lord, help them to survive and have a future
that is more than an empty, hopeless dream.

But Lord, you've shown me more than the burdens many
    humans bear.
I now know that new homes are rising from the rubble of
    District Six
in Cape Town, and that Mandela gave house keys not so long ago
to those who were evicted under white rule and their shameful
    use of power.
I've seen in other places not the use of power but of love:
in Kenya, where mission workers serve their people wisely
with counsel, leadership, patience, and winning kindness.
I've seen clinic workers reach out to their community,
often with no or little pay, few resources, and spare facilities.
I've seen widows take orphans into their huts and hearts,
and care for them, serving in the name of Christ, their only hope.

I've seen children in Christian orphanages laugh and play
and sing and dance, filled with the joy of living
in the midst of many desperate needs.
I've seen the glad anticipation of a far-flung community
waiting for the drilling of a well that would enable them
to grow their food and help provide their needs.
I've seen the gathering of wise tribal leaders and heard
their plea for help with AIDS and schools and crops,
and I've heard their fervent prayers, their songs of faith.
I've seen the Church at work, shared in the staff devotions,
and listened to their vision to work through local churches
and communities to make a difference that will last.
Dear Lord, thank you for all your faithful servants
that minister in Kenya and in the rest of Africa.

And show me, Lord, and all of us, what we can do
right where we are, to be your caring servants too.

☙ TO PONDER ❧

**A question for every day—what am *I* doing
for one in need?**

IN BUT NOT OF THIS WORLD

How then shall we live, dear Lord?

We, conceived and born in sin.

(Yes, Adam ate the apple, but our teeth still ache.)

We, with a natural tendency bred into our bone to ignore God
and neighbor.

We, doing the wrong thing so often, when we really want to
do the good.

We, wanting to hide our face when our faith proves fickle
once again.

> *…repent, embrace my mercy, take up your cross, and follow me…*

But how then shall we live, dear Lord?

In a culture that urges us to consume, consume, consume -- to
gratify ourselves (the economy depends on it); that wants us
to think that the good life is to have more than we need…

In a land where a child in his or her lifetime will consume as
many resources as 30 children born in India…

In an economy that sells us quality clothes at bargain prices
produced in sweat shops by the poor…

In a world where the chasm between the rich and the poor
widens steadily…

In a world where starvation, illiteracy, environmental
destruction, violent conflicts, and virulent disease are often
carelessly ignored or pronounced as hopeless…

In a world that in many places breeds despair and rage…

In a world where many feel increasingly alienated from each
other, from God, and from his creation…

How then shall we live in this world, dear God, as followers
of Christ?

> *…be very careful how you live…understand what the Lord's will is…*
> *…do not be conformed to this world…*
> *…be transformed by the renewing of your mind…*

…the one who does the will of God abides forever…

…the one who received the seed that fell among the thorns is the one who hears the word, but the worries of this life and the deceitfulness of wealth choke it, making it unfruitful…

…you cannot serve both God and Money…

…sell your possessions and give to the poor…

…where your treasure is, there your heart will be also…

…see to it that the light within you is not darkness…

…be imitators of God and live a life of love…

In a world where some nations are proud of their power, their wealth, their military prowess, while many others struggle to survive…

In a world where in some 3500 years of recorded history, fewer than 300 have seen no war…

In a world where we can't agree on a just cause for war or on the terror of its consequences…

In a world where weapons of mass destruction have been used by "us" and by "them"…

In a world where tyrants and terrorists try to overcome good with evil, and where good men, thinking that evil may be overcome with any means, discover that their good may become indistinguishable from the evil they set out to destroy…

In a world often more ready to shed the blood of its young than to pursue peace and preservation of life…

Oh God, how shall we live in this world as Christians?

…vengeance is mine…

…those who live by the sword shall die by the sword…

…do not repay evil for evil…

…overcome evil with good…

…love your enemy…

…do to others as you would have them do to you…

…follow peace with all men…

…blessed are the peacemakers…

…hear these words of mine and put them into practice…

Dear God, we repent of our sin, our failings, the weakness and
smallness of our faith.
We embrace your mercy with deep gratitude.
We want to be the followers of Christ in this world.
We pray for wisdom, for guidance, and for grace.
In Christ's name.

TO PONDER

**Do you sometimes feel, like Wordsworth, that "the
world is too much with us"?**

To Live By Faith

I think of them often, Lord—former team members, others, who
    returned to China, to teach English to eager students.

I think I know why they went back.
I've often had the yen myself.
It's why our missionaries keep going back.

It's being needed, Lord.
It's being there for those who want to learn not only, but who
    want to talk of burdens too great to bear alone; who need to
    know there's caring in a painful world; who need some hope
    when life is bleak or bitter; who are searching to save a life
    from insignificance—in China, or in Zuni, or in Uganda.

It's more than teaching English, then—or agriculture, or
    hygiene, or theology.
It's "teaching" Faith that counts the most to those who go in
    Jesus' name.
It's Faith that sends them back to mission fields where faith is
    daily prayed for, practiced, and proclaimed in acts and words
    of love.
I know, Lord, how the Spirit nurtures and shapes the Christian
    life in special ways when the main reason for being there is to
    exhibit the life of faith, in your face, your life, your love.

But that makes me wonder, Lord.
Why is that different in Grand Rapids than it is in Chengdu or
    Santiago or Kampala? Why is it harder to live by faith in the
    USA than it is in Santo Domingo?
Why is it less compelling to be a missionary in our church's
    neighborhood than it is in Pakistan?

I think I know something of the answer, Lord.
But help me to listen just the same.
Listen, and learn.

A TROUBLED WORLD

Dear God,

The world is not as it should be.

The children of Sarah and the children of Hagar are killing each other. Both call Abraham their father, but they call not on the heavenly Father for the spirit of peace.

In the land where the Prince of Peace was born, may hate give way to the hard work of forgiveness for the wrongs of the past. May people of good will reach across to each other and resolve to reason instead of shout, to pursue life instead of death, to do justice instead of violence.

No, God, the world is not as it should be.

Not in the Middle East, not in the Congo, not in North Korea, and not in so many other places.

Besides war, there's hunger, there's poverty, there's sickness for millions.

That's why we're pleading for healing in this broken world.

Oh God, have mercy.

But we would be wrong not to thank you, God, for the good that's in the world as well.

For an undivided Germany, a de-Stalinized Russia, a South Africa where Apartheid is no longer law.

For strong nations helping weaker ones with loans and food and goods.

For kings and queens, for presidents and premiers, for lawmakers and law enforcers who want to serve more than be served.

For peacekeepers. For earthkeepers.

For all the men and women who labor unselfishly for the good of others.

For the good earth that yields enough to feed its billions.

For places of searing beauty, of spine-tingling majesty, and of

such solemn serenity that for a moment we feel ourselves in
the presence of God.
For all this and more, we give you thanks.

Still, things are not as they should be.
Our own land of dreams has often been a cruel paradise.
There's so much that needs repentance, reform, and remedy…
in New York, in Washington DC, and in Grand Rapids too.
And in our church's neighborhood, our families, and me.
Forgive us, Lord, and help us face what's true:
that we are often weak, careless, or blind to our own vice.

But we also suffer when others hurt us willfully,
when they prove false in action and in word—
for all this and more, we pray your healing grace, dear Lord.

Help us to celebrate and build on all that's good,
to shun the wrong and do the things we should
in Jesus' name.

∼ TO PONDER ∼
What can *you* change that is not as it should be?

OH LORD, HAVE MERCY.

How precious is a human life?

Don't ask Dylan Klebold and Eric Harris. From the heart of darkness their voice would answer: it's worthless. The blackness of evil twisted their souls into demons of hate.

Don't ask the ethnic cleansers. They revel in making a hell for those judged unworthy of a place, of dignity, of life itself. As the devil's minions they rob and rape and kill because of race, or religion, or ethnic origin.

How precious is a human life?

Ask Police Sergeant J.C. Cosgrove. Words would fail him. The feelings are too strong. The feeling of great fear. For his daughter Lisa is inside the school where killers stalk and shoot to kill. His heart freezes at the real possibility of losing his child.

And the feeling of great love. When after agonizing hours of fear and prayer, Lisa comes running into her father's open arms, the heart is about to burst with such intensity of love that Sgt. Cosgrove will never look at his daughter again without remembering this moment.

How precious is a human life?

Ask Sabrije Rexhapi. Her answer would be tears. Tears flowing from a weeping heart whose every beat aches with love for her lost child. Serbs came suddenly, forced the family from their home, their town, their country. Twelve-year-old Adelina wasn't home when the Serbs came and thus was left behind. The uncertainty of her fate tears the mother apart. Where is her little girl now? What's happening to her? Is she safe? Will they ever see her again?

There's not a moment when Sabrije doesn't feel the craving of holding her child again, and the chilling fear that she may not.

How precious is a human life?

Ask anyone who has loved.

Ask God:
I have loved you with an everlasting love.
I lay down my life for the sheep.

"Love each other," you said, Lord.
Not taunt, abuse, or kill each other.
When will we learn in the Middle East, in Africa, in India?
When will we learn at our children's school and in our
    neighborhood?

Oh Lord, have mercy.

TRAVELING

This is my Father's world, and yes, I like to travel in it, to be in places far away and completely different from what I've grown familiar with.

I've been to a few such places, but too often played the part of a typical tourist there: the wide-windowed tourist bus, forty heads inside swinging right and left like metronomes as the guide points out noteworthy sites that were just passed; five-minute stops at scenic points to snap pictures as proof you've been somewhere; forty-five minute stops at shops for contributions to the local economy; ten-minute stops at monuments and cathedrals where local guides repeat their talk for the 1500th time to a crowd of curiosity seekers; the overnight stays in an American-like hotel where nearly everybody talks English and the dining room serves steaks and salads; and then the early bus ride or train ride or plane ride to the next spot, while faces and places and history flit by in blurred images that yield neither understanding nor memories.

The typical tourist travels to be able to say he's been to such a place or seen such a spectacle. Where they've been and what they've seen or heard rarely changes them, for they don't go to learn, to acquire a well-traveled mind; they merely exercise a well-traveled body.

Before I visit another place, I should like to fill my head about that place, and then fill my heart also when I am there. For though one takes a thousand pictures and stores them all neatly on a website gallery, if the storage chambers of the heart remain empty, all the pictures of our world are merely superficial show-off images on a screen.

Father, you know that the tourist mentality is not unfamiliar to our Christian life. Sometimes, too often, we think we have to fill our hours and days by trying to cram in as much as possible, unwilling to lose a chance at trying this, taking part in that, going here, stopping there, listening to one thing, watching another. Restless, we flit through life, haunted by the thought that we may not pass this way again. It is true that this is not our abiding place. But in our fear of missing anything, we miss it all.

Keep teaching us, Lord, that the value of our Christian life lies not in the quantity of our involvements but in the quality of our growth as children of God. The center of the Christian life is not the superficial sampling of a smorgasbord of blessings; it is more the celebration of creation and re-creation, the tending of the Garden, the care of its fallen, fragile creatures, and the preparation for the final feast.

When next I travel, I hope to be more of a visitor who is eager to savor more of his Father's world of rich diversity. I hope to linger a while in some places: to get a feel for its uniqueness, to listen and talk to its people, to observe their ways, to remember their history, to treasure their beauty, and to understand their needs. Maybe then good traveling, like good reading, will, in one writer's words, give us more to be Christian with.

Let it be so, Father.

⌒ TO PONDER ⌒
What experience gives *you* more to be Christian with?

Prayer for the Retirement Years

Dear Lord, help me to age with elegance
like good wine in, yes, old skin.
Help me to relish the lifting of the yoke
resting on my shoulders for so many years,
often most comfortably, thank God,
but sometimes more like a millstone 'round my neck.
Help me to glory in the freedom
to turn off time clocks
and catch those extra winks at last.

And Lord, help me accept that I
may not be sought out so much now
for my ideas and opinions.
Deliver me from the delusion that I
am irreplaceable, but also from the lie
that I am no longer needed.
I'd still like to be useful,
at least a little, Lord.
Show me your purpose
for this chapter of my life—
maybe to do some things I've always dreamed about,
to give my time without a paycheck for reward,
to go where I am needed,
where I can be a light or
give a cup of water in your name.
I can still serve through gifts
you've blessed me with,
and through my hopes and prayers
and those who took my place.
Help me discover, Lord, how life,
even at this stage, can quite unexpectedly
renew itself and surprise with joy.

Keep me from becoming a carping critic, Lord,
of those whose visions differ from my own
and change some things that I hold dear.
But fill me with the gift of praise
and move my tongue to bless the lives of those
who struggle and are burdened
with the sweet words of encouragement
that fall like sunshine on a frosty ground.

Lord, forgive me if only now, as I retire,
it dawns on me how much you love me
and how much you've blessed me in my life.
Now grow in me, oh Lord, a clearer,
deeper sense of joy for what is behind
and for what is yet to come.
Take my hand, Lord, and lead me
step by step along this way of growing old.
Fill me with steadfast faith and hope and love
through all the storms, and sunsets too,
till I have reached my final home,
my journey done, and safe with you.

‿ TO PONDER ‿
What are *your* hopes for the retirement years?

FAITH DURING DIFFICULT TIMES

*Life is seldom experienced as ideal, constantly
    tranquil and beautiful.*

"Wail, for the world is wrong," cried the poet.

*Perhaps Christians know the truth of that better
    than most.*

*We know that the most terrible things can happen
    to anyone.*

And that sometimes haunts us with fear.

Fear of losing a loved one.

Fear that love itself may die.

*Fear of so much more that would plunge our life
    in darkness.*

*And when bad things happen to good people, we
    cry out with the Psalmist:*

Where is God?

*But then, in the deepest, darkest valley—the
    profession of faith:*

The Lord is my shepherd... .

And because he is, the final destiny is Home.

DOUBTS

I asked them about their doubts, Lord. Their doubts were many and deep, and there was much pain in them. This is what they said.

"Jesus is supposed to love me, but I got my brand-new bike stolen when I was 10, I lost my sister in an accident when I was 13, and my parents divorced when I was 15. If I love somebody, I wouldn't let stuff like that happen to them."

"Faith is supposed to make people good and love each other. But, my dad drinks too much and fights with my mom. And my boss who's a Christian has a nasty temper. As far as I can see, people act the way they are, and faith makes no difference."

"Why should we believe in God, anyway. If someone tells you about an uncle on Mars for a dozen years or more, after a while you're gonna believe you have an uncle on Mars. And so long as you're with people who keep talking about that uncle, you'll think he's there. But you never see him and you can't go there to find out. And then you discover that most people think it's a fairy tale—there's no uncle; there's no God. I mean, I want to believe there is, but why should I—where's the proof?"

"God is supposed to hear and answer prayer. What prayers— for nice weather so the congregation can have a nice picnic together? For Aunt Sally to sell her house quick so she can go on a trip? For a peaceful solution to the Middle East crisis while we're divided bitterly on who bears the blame for the terrible enmity between Muslim and Jew? Well, did prayer make any difference? Does it change anything? Or is God just as deaf as the Baal of the Old Testament?"

"And what about miracles. God is supposed to have that power. We even pray for a miracle now and again. But I haven't seen any. I'll believe it when I see a tornado or typhoon level the mansions of the corrupt but cut a wide swath around the shacks of the pious poor. Or when cancer turns malignant only in the bodies of God-haters. Or when ravens come to feed the starving. As it is, it's easier to believe in an indifferent law of cause and effect."

And that was only the tip of the iceberg, Lord. But I'm glad they spoke. I think you love a doubter more than a hypocrite.

They want to believe, Lord, I am sure of that. They're searching, most of them, but they cannot find. They want no blind, unthinking faith, and they want no more pat answers to their questions. But they're hungry for Truth and for the gift of faith.

Help us to listen to them, Lord, and to be honest with them, as they are honest with us. Help us especially to share with them the miracle of grace—a transformed life.

⟿ TO PONDER ⟿
What questions do *you* find difficult to answer?

PRAYER

Dear Lord, do you listen to my prayers? I can't help wondering if
you hear me when I pray.
>*i haven't heard from you, my child*
>*have you been praying?*

Of course I have! Nearly every day! Why have you not heard me?
>*when do you pray?*

What does when have to do with it? Unless there are times of
day or night when you tune out.
>*no, my child, my ears are never closed*
>*when do you pray?*

Well, at meal times mostly. And not always then. Sometimes
before I go to sleep. Especially when I have a hard time falling
asleep. And in church, of course, with all the other people.
But you haven't heard me.
>*no, my child, i have not heard your voice for quite some time now*
>*i've been wondering why, and i've been waiting*

Well, I'm upset. What good is prayer if it goes nowhere, if like
breath it evaporates in air.

it's no good at all
>*tell me, what sort of things do you pray for when you pray, as you*
>*say, nearly every day*

The usual things, of course. For a blessing on the food, on
friends, on family, on sleep and rest, and for the problems of
the world—all the things we're supposed to pray for, right?
>*ah yes, of course*
>*tell me something: do you have a close friend?*

Yes, why do you ask?
>*do you talk together often, you and your friend?*

Of course, that's what friends do.
>*yes, right; and what do you talk about?*

Everything; we have that kind of relationship.
>*beautiful; and when there's trouble in your life, do you tell*
>*each other?*

Yes! We spend hours together sometimes when times are tough
and we need support.

> *yes, because you have a relationship*
> *are we in relationship too, my child?*

[*s i l e n c e*]

> *to pray is to be in relationship, you see*
> *a love relationship—with the Father, Son, and Holy Spirit*
> *do you see that prayer is more than saying some words at meal or*
> *bedtime?*

Yes, I think I'm beginning to. But I still have much to learn.

> *of course; all my children do*
> *in your heart, do you want a relationship with your Father?*

Oh yes, I think I do. But, but, will you help me?

> *that's a prayer I heard!*
> *and yes, I surely will!*

How do I begin?

> *by being honest with yourself and me*
> *by simply telling me what's on your mind, what's in your heart*

And what will you do?

> *I'll walk with you, love you, and help you find your heart's*
> *true home.*

∼ TO PONDER ∼

If praying is hard for *you*, what makes it so?

FEAR

I've known the ordinary fears of childhood:
the fear of losing what's needed
as a permanent possession: parents.
I feared when they quarreled.
I feared when Dad needed surgery.
I feared in occupied Holland when Dad
didn't come home and Nazis were everywhere.
I feared when Mom peddled her way through a
     spy-poisoned town,
saddlebags bulging with underground newspapers.
I feared when firebombs were bursting in air,
the sky lit up all around us, and homes were ablaze not far away.
I feared when Germans went from house to house looking for
     people in hiding,
and the man they wanted dead or alive standing beside me
     behind the window,
watching them come—
to be a child is a fearful thing;
to be a child in wartime is terrifying.

I've known the fears of a spouse:
the fear of losing an essential part of self.
I feared when accidents struck, when a cough hung on too long,
when waiting for the outcome of exploratory surgery at
     midnight.
I feared when stress and strain would sometimes take their toll,
and unloving words would fall like ice upon the heart—
to be a spouse is a fearful thing.

I've known the fears of a parent:
the fear of losing life's most precious possession.
I feared when the new-born baby's back was not closed
and too much fluid pressed upon the brain.
I feared when I sat with my six-year old in a hospital room

one long, dark night, his illness undiagnosed.
I feared when curfew struck and I hadn't heard a car
    come home.
I feared when the police came to church to tell us
there had been a roll-over and a closed head injury.
I feared when cold distance broke down communication
and no arms were long enough to reach across.
I feared when my daughter's husband betrayed
her trust and abused her love until it died—
to be a parent is a fearful thing.

But there are fears I have not known,
worse fears that tear the heart and scar the soul.
I've not known the fear of concentration camps.
I've not known the fear of floods sweeping loved ones away.
I've not known the fear of starvation nor of massacres.
I've not known so many fears that plague my fellowmen.
For all of us poor human beings are stalked by fear from birth—
to be born into a fallen world is a very fearful thing.

Perhaps, dear Lord, you know that best of all:
your fears turned sweat to blood
and faith to prayers to have the cup pass by,
and when the via dolorosa ended at Golgotha
there was no Peter, James, or John to give you aid,
no, not even God himself reached down to save his only son.

So, Lord, you understand why I'm afraid,
that I do fear "the terror by night
and the arrow that flies by day,
the pestilence that stalks in the darkness
and the plague that destroys at midday?"
For I know that the "rivers may sweep over me,"
That "the fires may burn me"—as they have
so many of your children.
But in my fears, Lord, will you hold me close?

For I, mere mortal, cannot endure the darkness
of God's absence, as you did upon the cross.
My Lord, my God, when fears fill and freeze my heart,
and evil's fangs bite deep into my soul—
then for my final peace may I hear and trust your word:

Fear not, for I have redeemed you;
I have summoned you by name;
You are mine.

TO PONDER

Do *you* have a fear that won't go away?

DEATH OF A MARRIAGE

I know those who've had to bury a husband or a wife, Lord. How heart-rending that must be to do! We feel it deeply bred into our bones that what you have put together is not meant to be sundered. From the beginning, death was not our destiny.

"Till death do us part" we say when flushed with the thrill of being united. We could as well say "till hell freezes over," so far is the thought of death removed from us on our wedding day.

But then comes a day when what was given is taken away, when those who love must do what is so very hard: to let go of one who has grown far more precious since those marriage vows were spoken. And when the grave closes on that person whose life became so inextricably tangled with one's own, it closes too on a part of self that cannot be the same without the other.

Oh God, how desperately difficult to bury one you love!

But Lord, how does one bury a marriage? There's nothing in the vows about divorce. A marriage is not expected to die. But it does—sometimes. In spite of denials. In spite of pleadings and prayers. In spite of extraordinary measures to revive, to save. It dies.

And there is no church ritual for a dead marriage. There is no funeral service. No calls of condolences. No mailbox stuffed with messages of comfort. No church family gathering around the grieving, hurting members with sympathetic tears and supportive hugs.

There are no Christian burial rites for a marriage. There's only a hostile courtroom and a legal document that nullifies the vows, the joy, the promise of the wedding day. And a silent bedroom to take the shattered dreams, the bloodied heart, the tormented mind. Alone. Alone.

No, a marriage is not supposed to die. Love is not supposed to die. There is so much that is not supposed to happen. But Lord, you know it does. And when it does, Lord, will you show us how to help each other?

FOR THOSE LEFT ALONE

"I pronounce you man and wife."

They had been man and wife for more than sixty years.
In all that time the romance had not died.
When they awoke each morning, side by side,
they faced and planned the day together, and it was good.
Love coursed through their bodies' blood,
they knew each other's feelings of the heart,
for what God had joined together had become one.

"Till death do us part."

It did. The good work of God undone by death.
A fleeting breath, eyes that close, and empty place.
Oh Lord, nothing makes us long more for kingdom come,
a final Home, than when our life is sundered from another,
who had made ours whole.

For how can love abide the final farewell death imposes,
after six or sixty years?
God made us for companionship, for life and love:
when these end, hearts break and drown in endless tears.

"Let not man put asunder."

In our fallen, painful world, that happens too,
another death that separates, that isolates the soul
before its God in desperate need of grace.

So we pray, dear Lord, for all who're left alone,
who miss the voice, the touch, the face
of one to rise with in the morning light,
with whom to plan and spend the day, to share the night.
Help us to understand how hard it is
to go to church alone, attend a concert,
savor a sunset, or a meal.

Help us to feel their hurt, to be there when they need us, Lord,
offer an empathetic word,
and be the channels of your grace.

∼ TO PONDER ∼
**How can we best treasure what we
don't want to lose?**

SAFE AND SECURE?

"I feel abandoned," I hear one say. "I feel betrayed," another.
"The world is not the same, it's become a colder, darker place."
"I don't see God's goodness; in fact, I don't see God at all."

I'm often haunted by those voices; and God, you must be too.
You heard them after 9/11; you heard them after a parent's
    suicide.
You heard them after the Slaughter of the Infants and the
    gassing of five million Jews.
You heard them, saw the light change in their eyes, and life's
    laughter fade.

Yes, I hear other voices too: the voice of faith that clings to God
when sorrows like sea-billows roll.
I've heard the voice of faith when, severely tested
in the crucible of a broken world, exclaim in praise
to God who did not withdraw the everlasting arms.
Its mystery never fails to move me,
this glimpse of heaven's kingdom, power, and glory.

But I think of those others now, those whom we have failed.
We tell them in Sunday School, maybe even in the pew:
God is all-powerful, compassionate, and good.
He takes care of you if you put your trust in him.
He is always in control, you never need to be afraid.
For God loves you; he won't let evil bring you harm.

And then we illustrate, through many a story,
the goodness, truth, and comfort of it all.

For, after all, we read in your own Word
that you, our God, will neither slumber nor sleep.
God, the Psalmist says, is our guard and our shade.
He watches over us and over all that he has made.

We need not fear the terror of the night,
nor the arrow that flies by day.
For he will command his angels to guard us in all our ways.

O God, you know how badly we want to believe that,
how much we need the comfort of knowing that it's true.
How much we love to read and sing of your special care
for those who love you and whom we love too.

But we remember: You didn't kill the Garden's snake.
You didn't prevent floods, or war, or droughts and famine.
You didn't cure Saul's paranoia, nor prevent David's sin.
You didn't save Christians from the lions or the sword.
You didn't even save your own Son from suffering and death.

No, God doesn't knock the gun from the killer's hand.
He doesn't disable the child abuser or the rapist.
He doesn't grant immunity to cancer or to fatal accidents.
He doesn't wrest away the cockpit controls from a terrorist.
He doesn't even change the figures that tell the IRS a lie.

When we ourselves are struck by some catastrophe,
the truth hits us like a bullet in the heart.
Then the abstraction becomes concrete:
Adam's fall afflicts us all.

Dear God, keep us from passing on illusions
that your children are safe and secure from all alarm.
Help us accept and preach and teach that we are not,
though you've got the whole world in your hands,
for evil in human hearts and deeds has consequence.

Of course, O God, we plead for your protection,
for miracles of healing, power, and peace.
And when, sometimes, you grant our prayer,
our faith soars, our trust again restored.

But more often, you do not.
Your children suffer, at times nearly beyond ability to bear.
Then they stare into the blackness of their soul
and ask, where is this God of might,
this God of goodness, loving care, and light?

Show us that, even then, we are not forsaken nor betrayed,
for all the martyrs are your holy evidence.

Help us to train our children's ears in faith, dear Lord,
to hear your voice, not in explanation of a mystery,
but a promise that rings true to a believer's heart,
and has the power to take us through the darkest night.

I am the good shepherd, I know my sheep...
I lay down my life for the sheep...
I give them eternal life, and they shall never perish;
no one can snatch them out of my hand...
no one can snatch them out of my Father's hand.
I and the Father are one.

Dear Lord, help us to believe.

⌘ TO PONDER ⌘
**Do *you* know someone who felt deceived
by childhood faith?**

PSALMS

To be human is to be vulnerable to affliction. Depression is a particularly insidious affliction. It has plagued young and old from the beginning of human history. The Psalms are a rich record of God's children crying out as they experience the valley of despair. The following fragments reflect a part of that record.

You made me trust in you, even at my mother's breast.
From birth I was cast upon you; from my mother's womb you
    have been my God.
You have been my confidence since my youth.

Answer me when I call to you, O my God, be merciful to me and
    hear my prayer,
for I am lonely and afflicted.
The troubles of my heart have multiplied; my soul is in anguish.
How long, O Lord, how long? I am worn out from groaning;
all night long I flood my bed with weeping and drench my couch
    with tears.
Listen to my cry for help; be not deaf to my weeping.
Awake, O Lord! Why do you sleep?
Rouse yourself! Do not reject me forever.
Why do you hide your face and forget my misery.
Rise up and help me because of your unfailing love.

My thoughts trouble me and I am distraught.
My heart is in anguish within me; it is blighted and withered
    like grass.
My strength is dried up like potsherd, sapped as in the heat
    of summer;
even the light has gone from my eyes.

Fear and trembling have beset me; horror has overwhelmed me.
I said, "Oh, that I had the wings of a dove!

I would fly away and stay in the desert;
I would hurry to my place of shelter, far from the tempest
    and storm."

My God, my God, why have you forsaken me?
Why are you so far from the words of my groaning?
O my God, I cry out day by day, but you do not answer,
by night, and am not silent.

I spread out my hands to you.
My soul thirsts for you like a parched land; my spirit faints
    with longing.
O Lord, do not forsake me; be not far from me, O my God.
Let the morning bring me word of your unfailing love, for I have
    put my trust in you.
Do not reject me or forsake me; come quickly to help me, O Lord
    my Savior.

Save me, O God, for the waters have come up to my neck.
I sink in the miry depths, where there is no foothold.
I have come into the deep waters.
Deep calls to deep in the roar of your waterfalls;
all your waves and breakers have swept over me.
I am confined and cannot escape; my eyes fail, looking for
    my God.
Why, O Lord, do you reject me and hide your face from me?
I am worn out calling for help; my throat is parched.
Rescue me from the mire, do not let me sink.
Do not let the floodwaters engulf me or the depths swallow
    me up
or the pit close its mouth over me.
Answer me, O Lord, out of the goodness of your love; in your
    great mercy turn to me.

I cried out to God for help; I cried out to God to hear me.
At night I stretched out untiring hands and my soul refused
    to be comforted.

My heart mused and my spirit inquired:
"Will the Lord reject forever? Will he never show his favor again?
Has unfailing love vanished forever?
Has his promise failed for all time?
Has God forgotten to be merciful?
Has he in anger withheld his compassion?"

(What a blessing when after a long darkness, the first
glimmers of dawn break through; when faith still seems possible.)

The Lord hears the needy. I am still confident of this:
I will see the goodness of the Lord in the land of the living.
Wait for the Lord; be strong and take heart and wait for the Lord.

Why are you downcast, O my soul? Why so disturbed within me?
Put your hope in God, for I will yet praise him, my Savior and
    my God.

You who fear the Lord, praise him!
For he has not despised or disdained the suffering of the
    afflicted one;
he has not hidden his face from him, but has listened to his cry
    for help.

(And when at last the sun reappears, it feels like a rebirth,
and groans turn into exclamations of gratitude.)

I love the Lord, for he heard my voice; he heard my cry for mercy.
The Lord is gracious and righteous; our God is full of compassion.
When I was in great need, he saved me.
He reached down from on high and took hold of me; he drew me
    out of deep waters.
You O Lord kept my lamp burning; you turned my darkness
    into light.

You turned my wailing into dancing;
you removed my sackcloth and clothed me with joy, that my
    heart may sing to you and not be silent.
O Lord my God, I will give you thanks forever.

Cast your cares on the Lord and he will sustain you.
His love stands forever; he will never let the righteous fall.

The Lord is my Shepherd.
I am always with you; you hold me by my right hand.
It is good to be near God.

KYRIË ELEÏSON

We are wanderers in the dark,
limited in thought, powerless in
deeds, signifying nothing in words.
We confess that often our eyes
cannot see the good, our ears are
deaf to the sounds of heaven,
our lips do not give praise, that
we are not your image-bearers.
Have mercy, Lord...

We are people of darkness:
Black is the day when madness
strikes, when even the light reveals
no purpose, no answers to the
question of existence, or to the
doubts that blinds our eyes.
Have mercy on us, Lord...

We are people of darkness
when there's no way out of pain
but only the void of indifference.
There is no hand that supports, no
eye that comforts, no word that
is gentle, no person to lean on.
Only you, Lord; we pray for mercy...

We are people of darkness
in our grief. We live with empty places
of loved ones lost. We live in
loneliness: the living pass us by,
the dead are our companions.
Who will come to us, who will bring relief,
who promises a future, who
opens windows to our sealed-in self?
May you be the one, O Lord...

We are people of darkness.
Many supplied, denied, and robbed
us of a god. We no longer know
what we believe, who you are,
if you don't come down to our
human foolishness, to our
cold hearts, to our confusion.
Show us your heart, O Lord...

We are people of darkness.
Be a light to us, O Lord...
Just through a crack, a hope
that grows and grows and...

translated and adapted from a
Frisian poem by Jan Dotinga

✧ TO PONDER ✧
What makes for darkness in *your* life?

EPIPHANY

You did not make us for the darkness, Lord, but for the light.

You said, when time began and darkness was upon the earth:
Let there be light!

In the deep midwinter, when nights are long and many days are
    without sun,
we long for light.
In our wrestling at the Jabbok, when no blessing and no
    daybreak come,
we long for light.
In the nightmares of our fears and losses, when we see no clear
    way out,
we long for light.
In the conflicts between nations, when hate's unleashed and
    snuffs out life,
we long for light.
In the arrogance of power, when puffed-up pride distorts the
    human heart,
we long for light,.
In the darkness of this season, and of our world, and our
    immortal souls,
we long for light.

Yes, God, we know the light has come,
and the darkness has not and will not overcome:
not the darkness of an absent sun,
not the darkness of a sunken spirit or a hurting heart,
not the darkness of prolonged grief or of searing memories,
not the darkness even of yet another war and deadly terrorism;
this is our faith, our comfort, and our hope.

For we have known the light to pierce our own dark places,
we've often seen the light in kindly words and loving deeds.

We know bearers of the light who've seen the desperate faces
of those in great distress, past tears, past hope, past prayers,
and pushed the darkness back, in Jesus' name.
We know that in your name, some hungry now are fed,
some homeless sheltered, some orphans cared for,
some lonely visited, some of the lowly lifted up.
We thank you, God, that evil can't destroy the good.

But Lord, there's so much darkness still,
in the human heart, and hence our world.

We long for the Star to lead us once again
to the place where God is still among us,
still for us, still teaching us and blessing us,
still healing us and loving us and saving us.

Dear God, in the darkness of our night,
may the work of sin and Satan cease.
Help us do justice, grant your peace,
speak your word once more: Let there be light!

COMFORTING THE SICK AND SORROWING

The Christian prays in praise when "God's in
his heaven and all's right with the world," as
Robert Browning put it.
The Christian prays in agony when God seems
absent and the world's falling apart.
A hospital room can be a fearful place, and a
funeral home can break your heart.
But among the fearful and the mourning,
the Lord comes
"to bring good news to the afflicted, to bind up the
brokenhearted,
to comfort all who mourn... ."
And we, his disciples, do the same,
in his name.

HOSPITAL PRAYERS

They're not like other prayers.
They're short, intense, pointed.
The outside world retreats.
There's only the person in OR, in ICU,
Who represents the entire world that matters.

> Oh God, spare him.
> Dear Lord, keep her heart beating.
> Loving Shepherd, carry your precious sheep safely through this valley.
> Please bless the doctors and nurses with skill and success.
> Oh God, listen to our prayers; don't leave us now!

And the person in the bed?
Incoherent snatches, maybe.
Maybe none at all.
When the feeling of sickness, of total discomfort, of constant pain and nausea and anxiety permeates,
there's only coping left, from minute to endless minute.
God is not in those minutes.
The person is alone, much as Christ was alone in the agony of the crucifixion.
In the deepest darkness of the valley, a person walks alone.

Only when awakening from a morphine-induced sleep,
an overwhelming sense of God's presence may return
and fill with gratitude.
Until the morphine wears off and the body resumes its rebellion.

No, God is no morphine.
He's not a magic potion that drips into our veins with instant healing power.
But God is in the morphine and in the IVs and in all the tubes that connect the body to machines.
And God is in the prayers.

The urgent prayers of family by the bedside.

The daily and nightly prayers of family and friends elsewhere
and the faithful all around.

Those prayers descend like manna on those pleading for hope
and healing.

In those prayers God's presence is constant, even through the
darkest valley, and in each agonizing moment of distress.

Such prayers support those prayed for as surely as they bless
those who pray.

Blessed are those who pray, for God is listening.

⤜ TO PONDER ⤛
Do *you* ever feel that God isn't listening?

PRAYER OF THE INCURABLY ILL

There are words that freeze the blood, that chill the bone:
I'm afraid I have bad news...

   ...it's inoperable...

   ...it's a progressively debilitating disease...

   We don't know the cause, and there is no cure...

   We can fight it for awhile but, except for a miracle, we can't
      win...

Oh Lord, you know us who've heard such words. You know how
   those words turned dreams to dust, turned faith to fear.

We no longer ask "why," Lord—why some should live so long
   that they long for death, while others vibrant with life and
   purpose should be struck down. We're tired of the "whys"
   that go nowhere, that ring their hollow echoes in our souls.
   Even your agonized "why" from the cross went unanswered.

No, we don't expect explanations on demand. You owe us none.
   And we realize that a tortured heart hurling its challenges at
   heaven's door is hardly receptive to divine reasoning, even if
   it should be given.

What we need, Lord, what all of us need, is to know that you're
   not absent even when you're silent. We need to know that
   bad things happening to good people do not signify your
   indifference.

We don't insist on answers, Lord. We pray for your presence.

Oh Lord, you are acquainted with grief.

You know that hands must often ball up into fists before they
   can fold in prayer.

You know that voices must often rage before they whisper their
   faith.

You know that often the torments of despair must wrack the soul
before it can embrace your love.

Let us know your presence, Lord, inside those shadows of the
valley, and hold us close.

When sleepless eyes stare into the haunting blackness of past-
midnight hours, show yourself and turn the darkness
into light.
When pains torture the body, may the grace of your presence
prove sufficient.
When the humiliation of dependence shatters dignity, may
the pressure of your everlasting arms assure us that we are
precious in your sight.
When waves of fears for self and loved ones threaten to swallow
the tempest-tossed, walk those waves with us and turn terror
into peace.
When the sufferings and limitations of this mortal flesh defeat
us, remind us that glory waits.

Lord, walk with all of us who are smitten.
Through your presence restore our faith.
Through your promise, rekindle our hope.
Through your love, enlarge and perfect the love that casts
out fear.

Nothing can separate us from the love of God
that is in Christ Jesus our Lord.

✑ TO PONDER ✑
What do *you* fall back on when bad things happen?

LIFE'S DIRTY TRICKS

"I've got to make a phone call tonight,
and I don't know what I'm gonna say."

His face across from me was troubled.

"What kind of call are you talking about?"

He pecked away at his food before he answered.

"My wife called.
One of my colleague friends is in the hospital.
They found cancer near his spine; inoperable.
They give him less than twelve months to live."

I was silent. I remembered that not so long ago
my own friend and colleague
received his death sentence: a brain tumor
that would take his life within the year.

He continued, voice bitter with irony.
"Dan planned to retire early,
enjoy some traveling while his health was good.
What will I say to him.
What can anybody say.
It's just one of life's dirty tricks."

The Hemingway line struck me.
Life often seems to play its cruel games with us:

A child goes to the store on her new bike.
She never comes back.
She's found later, raped and choked to death.

Love between parents wanes, grows cold, and dies.

Children are bewildered and feel betrayed.

A father in the prime of life collapses on the job.
The family will never feel his embrace again.

The phone rings in the night:
"There's been an accident;
your son was killed."

These are but a few of "life's dirty tricks."
They leave us in the dust, weak and trembling.
We can lose anything at any time:
health, mind, friends, parents, children,
husband, wife, jobs, strength, even faith.

Oh Lord, it seems so wrong.
We were created for the Garden, not the grave.
How do we harmonize life's dirty tricks
with a good God's providence and promise
that "all things work together for good."

Job knew much about suffering.
He could not understand the reason.
To our finite minds, it makes no sense.
We know this: Satan uses our afflictions
to his own demonic ends,
hoping that by the loss of one of God's good gifts
we might also lose our souls.
But Job did not curse you, Lord.
He humbled himself when he encountered you
and learned that God's ways are past finding out.

And there is something else,
as incomprehensible as the suffering
of Job and Jesus and Paul: grace.
In the end, his grace is sufficient,
as all the saints will testify.

It has power to turn grief into hope,
turmoil into peace,
doubts and questions into praise.

I don't know what my friend told his that night.
But I know that if one's sight
includes no vision
beyond the torments and trials of our life,
one can only echo Frederic Henry's summation
of his still-born child and dying wife:
"It's just a dirty trick."

⁓ TO PONDER ⁓

What loss would be the hardest to bear for *you*?

WHY?

It's springtime,
a cardinal sings and the scent of roses is in the air,
the fountain splashes, the bees drone
and the sunshine is everywhere.

One of my friends will get a ring
another will marry soon.
My mother's dead
my father's an M.D.
who's supposed to heal,
but I'm in bed
and I'm dying!

My father says: Do you hear the cardinal,
here, here's a rose, my child, how are...?
I smile: Fine, father.

How can I say: Please make me well,
when I see the pain deep in his eyes.
He would give his life for me,
but of course that cannot be.

One did give His life for me, I'm told,
yet must think it better now
that I not live but die.
He apparently approves
the death of my spring blossom
from an icy winter cold.

Oh God, I scream to you my
Why?

I want to live another spring
and summer too.

How can I die
when cardinals sing
and roses smell?

The whole long, glorious day
I rage against disease,
but when evening shadows fall
I still have not reached peace.
Dead-tired from all my darkling thoughts,
I tear away for some diversion.
Soon the screen flickers through the gloom
and a choir sings: "I do not ask you why."
Faces devout, eyes softened,
they sing, "I do not ask you why"!
No, not they, they face no doom,
but what about me who's going to die?

Angry, I turn off the light
and mouths on mask
and pious words all slide away,
the words I cannot sing.
Don't we all have our "why" to ask?

At my wit's end, I take His book
which does not lie
and read the all-familiar words.

I skipped right over them when I was well,
Oh, I believed them, Lord.
But now in my own private hell
I must believe they are Your Word.

It's not enough to be resigned
to an inevitable fate.
I must accept, even approve,
in spite of all that's wrong,

all my unanswered prayers,
my innumerable "whys".

He says:
"Why do you sigh,
'my path is hidden from the Lord
and my cause escapes his eye?'
Am I not He who makes the weary strong,
who makes the grieving glad
and turns death into eternal spring?
Try me, I am He who keeps His word!"

And now I cannot help myself,
I simply yield,
and whisper:
It is good,
I don't know why,
but it is good,
because you say it is!

When my father returns late that night,
he sees that I've been healed
unto eternal life.

—translated and adapted
from a Frisian poem by Rens Woudstra

THE LAST SUPPER
IN MEMORY OF BOB DE HAAN

They were together for the final time,
gathered in the spacious upper room to share a special meal.
The sacrificial lamb they would feed on had been prepared.
He had been eager to celebrate Passover with them one last time.
For he knew his death was near.
He looked at those he'd known for the last three years.
He'd summoned them, led them, taught them, prayed for them.
And as he looked at each one's face, his heart was stirred.
They had become his family, and he loved them.
Now he was preparing to die for them.
He took the unleavened bread and broke it.
Then he fed them: this is my body given for you.
He offered them the wine: my blood poured out for you.
They ate, they drank, but did not understand his words.
The flesh had not yet been pierced, the blood not shed.
The cross not raised, with their Rabbi nailed to it.
Only then would they know that after their Seder meal
Jesus went out to die.
His body would be broken, his blood pour out for them.
Then they would weep with grief and gratitude.

Bob also knew his death was near.
He welcomed the sacrament one last time,
through bread and juice to share communion
with Roberta, the one great love of his married life,
and others gathered in the small hospice room on this winter day.
Surrounded by those he loved and who loved him,
dear sisters, nephews, pastors, church elders, friends,
Bob remembered the broken body and the shed blood,
as he had so many times before, but different now.
Bob knew that even as his own body was breaking down,
his breathing labored and his voice almost silent now,
the Lord's broken body would make him whole.

In his heart he joined us as we sang,
"How firm a foundation…"
He had come through fiery trials, and deep water,
the grace all sufficient his ample supply.
Now he was nearing the other side,
confident that he who had been forsaken
would never, no never, no never forsake.

A few days later, Bob gently breathed his last.
Then he was with God.
And we weep with grief and gratitude.

In Silence

I live in silence
though there are words
and many mouths
that open shut open shut
but make no sounds
that I can hear.

I live in silence.

For me no Handel
and no Mozart,
no Beethoven,
and no Bach.
Nor can I sing
as I once did.

I live in silence.

But I can receive the kindness
in another's eyes,
the beauty of spring skies
peonies preparing to unfold,
the sun,
the lake,
and the promise:

then shall the ears
of the deaf
be unstopped!

Hallelujah!

—translated and adapted from a poem by Rens Woudstra

MADE FOR DEATH?

You shall surely die!

But we were not made to die.
Garden memories still float within our soul
and of the Word that gave us life
of God who in eternity we were to worship and enjoy.
It's true we fell into the dark of night:
we ate the poison of mortality,
and hence we "rage, rage against the dying of the light"
and curse grim Death as our worst enemy.

We were not made to die.
You cried, Lord, when your friend had died.
Do you hear our sobbing in the night?
We crave to be with those we love
to feel their touch, their voices in our ears
their life enriching ours, in this world of blight
do you feel our hurting hearts, our burning tears?
do you cry when our loved ones die?

He has sent me to bind up the brokenhearted
to comfort all who mourn.

We were not made to die.
Death is the silence of the heart
the shutting of the mouth and eye
the closing of a casket, grave, and life
death turns to stone the living flesh
to memory the touch, the smile, the look
it leaves an empty chair, a vacant bed, an unread book
it is the final exit through death's dark door
it leaves a void where there was none before.

You have a high priest who is touched
with the feeling of your infirmities.

We were not made to die.
We fear that solitary path
that final journey to eternity
for those we love and for ourselves
we fear the torments of disease
the indignity of absolute dependency
we fear pursuing demons that indict
us for our blindness, sins of pride
our selfishness, our rank unworthiness
exposed in God's penetrating light
to holy scrutiny and righteous wrath
thus we cannot "go gentle into that goodnight."

> *I love you*
> *I gave my life for you*
> *if you believe in me*
> *you will not perish*
> *but have everlasting life.*

We were not made for death.
We belong, beyond our gasping breath
to our faithful Savior Jesus Christ.
Lord, when we approach death's shadow
grant us grace to know your presence
that takes away our fears, our tears,
that never ceases to surprise
by joy, that gives the quiet confidence
in him who has promised:

> *lo*
> *I am with you always*

> *My Father's will is that everyone*
> *who looks to the son*
> *and believes in him*
> *shall have eternal life*
> *and I will raise him up*
> *at the last day.*

THOSE WHO MOURN

Blessed are those who mourn...

"Blessed," Lord? Abel's family when Cain in cold blood cut down the life of this good man?

Jacob when his sons told him of the loss of his beloved Joseph?

David when he lost his best friend Jonathan? When he lost Solomon, his dearest son?

"Blessed," Lord? The husband whose wife was brutalized by fiends and dumped like garbage in a muddy pond?

The parents who've seen their children starve before their helpless eyes?

The mother whose young daughter was gunned down on a city street by an indifferent assassin who relished his power to kill?

The family who lost their father to a heart attack when they still needed him so much?

The wife whose dreams of retirement joys shattered when her husband died at 65?

The couple who lost each other through divorce that scarred their life?

"Blessed," Lord? Those whose hearts are riven with the pain of loss?

Those who prayed and begged, and yet disease and pain and death would not vanish like Näaman's leprosy?

Those who sit on the ash heaps of their loss and cry for what can never be again?

Those who feel the ache of absence undiminished in all the years that follow at those moments when a face, a voice, a footstep bring back memories of all that has been lost? Or when a place or time of special joy cries out to be shared with him or her who is no more?

Why "Blessed," Lord? When often they feel so robbed, so
cursed, even God-forsaken? Why "blessed," Lord?
...for they shall be comforted.

So, that's it, then. The blessing lies in comfort, not in grief.
"Comfort ye my people," God said, "comfort all that mourn."
The Son of God came, suffered, died, and rose again.
And through him, the God of heaven and earth leans down to a
    weeping child and shows pity.
The Lord of eternity reaches out to a hurting child of time,
    whispering infinite tenderness:
    *...I understand your sorrow...I love you with an everlasting love...I will
        stay close to you...let me share your burden, your pain, your fears...
        let me wipe your tears...*
    I have a place for you...
The blessing of divine comfort! The power of grace flowing from
    the Father to his child, making all things new again!

Bless the mourning among us, Lord, through the gift of your
    transforming comfort...through the gift of Easter life.

⟨ TO PONDER ⟩
What has been most painful in *your* life?

Going Home

This is the story of Beth.
Not the whole story; a person's life cannot be told in a page
   or two.
Like the heart of a mountain, there is always something beyond
   reach that remains.

Beth was still a child when she would hear her mother cry and
   her father leave.
Deep into the night she heard their quarrels.
She wanted and needed to love both Dad and Mom.
But she could not love her father. She blamed him for her
   mother's misery.

One day her father did not come back. And then the house she
   was born in ceased to be home.
She and her siblings began to live their separated lives, with
   grandparents, with uncles and aunts, from one to the other.
   Beth would often see her mother, but not her sister or her
   brothers. She never saw her father again.
But her Father in heaven was never far away. Her faith grew and
   the desire to serve him.

In time she found work in the city, met a man, and married.
   She tried to be a good wife more than he tried to be a good
   husband. She would have been a good mother too, but she
   never bore a child.

She found fulfillment in her church as elder and outreach
   worker. She showed great compassion to those who had
   no home and little happiness. She brought a ray of light to
   people and places sunk in darkness.
In her own house she served her husband who had become
   disabled and grown irritable. Yet she never complained; but
   what was deep within her heart no one ever knew.

Then Beth felt herself plunging into the blackness of night. She
   had cancer. And it was terminal.
Something deep within the core of her being snapped.
None, perhaps not even Beth herself, knew just what and why.
But in the blackness of her nights she screamed her pain
   and rebellion.
She struggled not with God—he seemed absent—but with the
   hell-sent demons of terror and despair.
This lasted for months.
She did not, she could not accept that her life should come to
   such an end.
Her tormented spirit writhed in anguish even as her body,
   wracked with pain and ineffectual medicine, grew grotesque.

At last she could struggle no longer.
Exhausted in body and soul, she grew silent. She would talk to
   no one.
Until one twilight evening, she asked her sister to sing a song she
   had always loved:
Jesus, Lover of My Soul.
And there, in the shadows of the darkening room, her sister who
   had not sung a song of faith since her childhood years, took
   Beth's hand and in unwavering voice sang the words that
   came back to her from so many years before:

> Jesus, Lover of my soul,
> Let me to thy bosom fly,
> While the nearer waters roll,
> While the tempest still is high!
> Hide me, O my savior, hide,
> Till the storm of life is past;
> Safe into the haven guide,
> O receive my soul at last!

Both sisters were silent; there was only the ticking of the clock,
   measuring mortality, the only sound seemingly in a universe
   where suns flamed and stars wheeled and constellations
   fell apart.

But then as inexplicably as the darkness descended, the light
from eternity broke through, strong and steady, till there was
no darkness left.

"I'm going home," Beth whispered.

Then she died.

Like Beth, we too are children of the light.

Still, we often walk in darkness, only faint flickering occasionally
illuminating the way.

We walk that road together, though we may feel so very much
alone.

But no road can lead us to a place where the grace of God cannot
touch us.

Even the road that descends into the blackest of nights
will lead us Home.

CELEBRATIONS

There is indeed the weight of disease and death that
*   burdens us.*
There is also much beauty that calls for celebration
*   and praise:*
the change of seasons
the gifts at harvest time
the union of two lives in love
the glow of health and happiness
the places that give peace and joy
the completion of a task well done—
for all this our spirit soars
and exclaims its thanks to God.

WINTER

Lord, in large parts of your world there is winter for every
    summer.
For every springing up of new life, there's a falling and a fading.
Followed by winter, the burial of leaves and seeds, the long rest
    in bleakness.
The summer frenzy of life slows down, the frozen air is still, and
    thoughts turn inward.

Maybe winter is for the young and hardy, who mind not bone-
    chilling cold.
They celebrate when there's snow to pack, ice to skate,
    mountains to ski.
And true, there's beauty in fresh snow on evergreens glistening
    under a winter sun.
And charm in telling stories around a blazing fireplace on a cold
    wintry night.

But for many there are too many gray, gray days without the sun.
And the nights so long, so cold, so dark.
We pray your mercy on those who have no home, no heat to keep
    them warm.
And on all who grow impatient, despondent, and wonder if
    spring will ever come.

And Lord, as our longing intensifies for spring to birth,
so may our longing grow for living in your Light.
As we long to see the daffodil emerge from earth,
so may our lives reflect our own emerge from spirit's night.

➤ TO PONDER ➤
What is winter's peculiar beauty for *you*?

MESSENGER OF SPRING

Our robin didn't come to our window this spring.

For several years in succession, spring's first robin would awaken us at dawn by his insistent tapping, tapping on our bedroom widow pane. Even when we lived on a San Juan island one sabbatical spring, "our robin" came to announce that the business of spring was underway.

I must admit that at 5:30 in the morning, the message was not kindly received. I was still in my winter sleep, and I resented the interruption by a foolish robin fighting a phantom enemy in the mirror of our bedroom window. And at that hour I was not yet ready to be impressed by the fact that Mr. Robin had reached his ancestral home after winging hundreds of hazardous miles from warmer climes, impelled by his urgency to stake out a homestead for a future family.

But I am the foolish one, I think. For the migration of the robin is America's most jubilant rite of spring. To be asleep when life awakes, to be unseeing when nature's first green turns gold, to be unhearing when the robin's song tunes the orchestra of spring is to deprive oneself of ecstasy. I think now the robin tried to tell me that nature's artist means to teach neither music to the deaf nor painting to the blind.

For spring is the sacred season when we ought to celebrate the promise of perpetuity. When spring breezes unglue the artfully folded buds and lilacs everywhere, when the tuneless cries of crows sound above the naked fields and new lawns are proudly wearing April's deep green and "the world is puddle-wonderful," the doxologies should spring spontaneous from every human heart in tune with God's good earth and responsive to his promise that

while the earth remains,
seedtime and harvest,
and cold and heat,
and summer and winter,

and day and night
shall not cease.

God of creation's spring, we tend to grow used to everything,
even spring perhaps. It often tiptoes in, belying the power that
"through the green fuse drives the flower." The slow-motion
explosion of germinating life all around us does not burst
forth with the sound of an earthquake, though its effect is far
more awesome. Yes, Lord, we need a robin to alert us to the
transforming power at work, to the grace of the Spirit's warm
breast brooding over winter's bent world and releasing the life of
"the dearest freshness deep down things."

Our robin did not come back to our window this spring, but
I'd like him to know, wherever he is, we got his message just the
same.

Praise to you, Creator God!

∽ TO PONDER ∽
Why is the arrival of spring so special to so many?

NEW LIFE

My God, it stuns us every time.

How the angels must've cart-wheeled through the heavens
when on Creation Day the world was born.

I remember Milton's Satan nearly mesmerized
when he first spied Adam's radiance down below.

I think of Noah's joyful urge to build an altar
when a wave-washed earth began to bloom again.

And how poor Mary Magdalene could not believe her ears
when her Rabboni called her name on Resurrection Day.

Then there was Paul of Tarsus, entering Damascus as a
    blinded fool,
till the scales fell from his eyes, and he saw all things as new.

One week, not long ago, before the house, a giant pile of snow.
The next, under a transforming sun, nature's first green
    springs out,
dry, brittle twigs swell strong with sap,
and skinny branches sport their tiny buds.
Lo, winter has passed, and the Garden, again, will grow.

My God, yes, it stuns us every time!
And in this our awakening hour,
we give glory, glory, glory to your all-creating power!

No, this is not a God-forsaken place,
for still in lives and nature
we see the beauty of your face.

But now, dear Lord, if small seeds can grow into huge fields
    of wheat,

into a tiny baby or a mighty people more numerous than
　　the sand,
if even what has died can throb with life again—
then cannot that same awesome might make a cold heart melt,
infuse a dying marriage with new life and love,
turn gnawing doubts into rich deeds of faith,
and lift the burdened soul to a closer walk with God?

So let it be, dear Lord, so let it be…
for Jesus' sake.

To Celebrate

"For, lo, the winter is past…"

if you made us for joy and laughter
for reveling in the sheer force of life
that has exploded all around us
for shouting and dancing at the boldness of the first daffodil
and gasping in wonder at the delicate temerity of the
early trillium
and the blossoms of a thousand cherry trees by Grand
Traverse Bay
for inhaling deeply the smell of fresh-mown grass
and the pungent fragrance of the lilac bush
for the beauty of the lilies that speckle the marshy rim of
Otsego Lake
and the bewitching patterns of Petoskey stones

if you made us for running the dunes at Sleeping Bear
feeling the warm beach sand slip through our toes
for hearing the shrieks of hawks soaring on dune thermals
for traveling the winding road past hidden coves
and deserted bays through the Hiawatha Forest
for gazing at the breath-taking beauty from the top of
Castle Rock
and camping amidst the quiet, rugged beauty near Paradise

if you made us for taking a book to the shores of a placid lake
for pausing on a bike ride in a sleepy village that forgot to rush
for fishing the Au Sable or floating down the Rogue
for a picnic on a Lake Huron beach
and a hike in the wildness of the Porcupines

if you made us, dear Lord, to enjoy our Maker
to celebrate these gifts of a lavish creation
if the thanks in our hearts gives glory back

to the Giver of new flowers and the songs of birds
then thank you, God, for this spring and summertime!

but even as we embrace these gifts with gladness
help us to remember that you made us too
to be present with those whose joy in life has faded
who fear the future, whose hearts are sad
who need our help, especially in summertime!

in all our joys this summer
we want to be fully alive to you
to your world in its beauty
and in its need
for Jesus' sake.

∼ TO PONDER ∼

Where are *your* favorite summer places?

SUMMER BEAUTY

Lord, in world marred by the ugliness of evil,
open my eyes, my ears, my heart
to the summer beauties of our life.

In a world where a century worth of industrial muck
lies at the bottom of our lakes and streams,
let me thrill to the pure beauty of the lone fisherman
softly rowing in the twilight toward shore
until the darkness gathers him in
and I hear only the gentle plash of waves.

In a world of noise and frenzy,
let me relish the beauty of a slow summer evening
lingering quietly under the backyard trees
while cardinals perform the evensong
and morning glories prepare for night.

In a world of mostly valley living and summer heat,
let me revel in the beauty of the mountain—
smelling its virgin breath of pines
hearing its welcome song in the gurgling sound of brooks
seeing the light careening on the waters of a mountain stream
feeling the cool spray of mist on cheeks and lips
from a gushing waterfall,
and then, the water pelting on my skull,
like a wakeup call from heaven,
exploding every fiber into glorious attention.

In a world of too many parched lands and barren deserts,
let me rejoice in the beauty of the Midwest
where double-ribboned freeways flow silent-gray
between squared-off fields abundant with tasseled corn.

Lord, though I know the shadow of death hovering
above all living things, let me see and celebrate,

with the wide-eyed wonder of infancy still within,
this summer world of beauty, the good green earth
renewed and ever renewing,
world without end!
For this is my Father's world,
created not in jest but in divine earnest
by a power full of unfathomable mystery and holiness.
Thine is the kingdom
and the power
and the glory
forever!

✐ TO PONDER ✐

How do *you* celebrate summer?

Summer Memories

Thank you, Lord, for summer.
It's past now, but the blessings linger, like the smell of
bacon in the early morning campground air.
Sure, there's been the irritation of sticky clothes,
sunburn, and mosquito bites.
But there's also been the pleasure
of walking through a sprinkler when the sun beat down
of drinking a tall cool glass of iced tea after a three-mile jog
of mountain hikes and ferry rides and campfire night
of cold fried chicken from a picnic basket
and fish frying on the grill at family reunions
and the fresh sweetness of the first corn cob
and the first green beans and carrots
from the well-tended garden plot
of the tennis racket swing and watching the ball
kiss the baseline for a winner
and the hit that drove in the winning run
for the church league team
of the blackberry stains on hand and face
that smell too good for washing
of shooting stars and fireflies
on a midnight walk.

Thank you, Lord, for summer,
for its gifts have made us glad.
Soon, colder winds will blow,
and leisure moments will accelerate
to a more hectic pace.
May summer time still play its music in our soul,
its timeless quality take us through falling leaves
and winter storms and messy thaws of spring,
its gentle grace flowing through our lives this year,
like a peaceful brook through a rocky land.

Autumn Joy

Autumn is flying her flags again
among the sugar maples of Vermont,
the golden cottonwoods in Zion,
the aspens in Colorado,
and all across the nation,
calling out to us, with seeing eyes
and eager souls to join the celebration
and glory in God's good creation.

But autumn is also Nature's funeral procession,
with intimations of our own mortality,
of the "blight man was born for."
The fire-jewels dangling from the red maple's branches
and the crimson rubies of the sumacs
will soon fall down.
And in their fall we see our own,
for, as Rilke reminded us,
"all have this falling sickness."

Autumn is a time of season-turning
that prods our soul to introspection,
a time to rake our leaves of unforgotten slights,
of loving self more than our neighbor,
and of so much imperfection—
then pile them high for burning.

Autumn is the season for faith:
to look at falling leaves
and see the blessing of rest
and the rightness of endings.

Autumn is the season for hope:
to look at trees that are now stripped bare,
at dreary days of rain and snow and slush,

and see beyond them to another season
of re-awakenings and new life everywhere.

That's why we embrace autumn with joy:
because of its brightness and its beauty,
because of "One whose hands we can't fall through,"
because of its promise of another time to come
with no more falling leaves or falling hands,
in heaven and earth that are forever new.
Praise God for autumn joy!

⌒ TO PONDER ⌒
**Do *you* feel "intimations of mortality"
when leaves fall?**

FALL FOLIAGE

In October every hill of flame calls us to attention.
The feastly foliage stirs our blood.
On a rare, crisp, and cloudless October day
we should go roaming and discover sumacs
like savages in war paint surround a country barn.
How not see the clear yellows and bright orange beckoning
through the deep crimson of the maple leaves
and hedgerows burn with a low running fire of blueberry bushes
and craggy oaks against the pale-blue October sky
playing out the colorful climax of the great autumn drama.

Or push through some sandy dunes where the lake comes
     foaming up the beach
and taste its fresh breath and hear its roar fill up the
     painted woods
then we'll know we're in the season and the place
where summer dies in glorious pageantry.

Something about autumn reaches deep down inside,
something that stirs us with mystery but with power too.
There's its beauty: bright colors flashing, twisting in the breeze
and its playfulness: the leaf, like an autumn-day child in gaudy
     yellow rain slicker chasing another down to its fading
     grassy grave.
But there's also a note of sadness creeping in
a "grieving over Goldengroves unleaving."
And deep down we feel the intimations of our mortality.

It's not forever springtime, and we're not forever young.
"To everything there is a season," said the Preacher:
a time to plant and a time to pluck up…
a time to be born, and a time to die."
And God-colored fall foliage so bright
that we cannot think of it as final blight.

That is the mystery and power of our faith, our hope and joy, as Mildred Zylstra put it in her "Autumn" poem:

The lily bulb is buried deep in earth.
Onion-layered skins, brown-tissue thin,
Will crumple off.
Green shoot emerge, tall stem,
White bell will ring out joyfully
In blue spring sky
With tongues of gold.

This fragile sheath of skin,
Brown-spotted, wrinkled flesh,
Will shrivel up.
What flower, with what form
Will blossom forth in unknown joy
In new spring sky
Only the Gardener knows.

✐ TO PONDER ✐
Which season exercises *your* faith the most?

THE LORD OF MARRIAGE

I don't know how many weddings you attended, Lord. In Galilee,
    I mean.
I'd think, though, after that sensation in Cana, you'd be a
    popular wedding guest.
Fathers of the bride would vie for your services.
After all, turning water into wine would knock a big chunk off
    the total wedding tab.
But we don't read of any repeat performance.
Maybe you sent your regrets to all the invitations?

I hope you still get invited to lots of weddings.
There's been a spate of them again this summer.
And I hope you sent regrets for none!
For what's a wedding without the presence of the Lord of wine,
but especially the Lord of Love?
Where does love come from if not from the Maker
of man and woman, whom he meant to become one flesh.
And when He gave one to the other,
I can imagine that the Creator himself threw Adam and Eve
a Garden Party that's never been equaled in extravagance of
    sheer beauty and loveliness.

So when bride and groom vow to love each other,
to honor and respect each other,
to serve and support each other—
what would be the weight of all those wonderful words if not
    said in the name of the Lord?
I hope you were the unseen Host at lots of weddings, Lord.

But when a wedding is over, marriage begins, even when there's
    a honeymoon.
Two lives trying to become one.
Not exactly like two streams coming together to form one river.
Not exactly like two lumps of clay kneaded into one.

More like a pair of horses harnessed together to pull the
    same carriage.
Or two people trying to row the same boat as a team.
That takes some learning!
That's when those wedding vows get tested.

For Lord, you do not expect the two to no longer be themselves.
Rather, that they, as themselves, learn to be husband and wife,
building a relationship, and a life, which reflect the Lord of Love
    and Life.
May they remember, Lord, that truly loving each other must be
    learned anew each day,
love that will override the differences that inevitably surface,
love that will not be waylaid by personal pettiness or a fault-
    finder's tongue.

We long for an ideal world where all vows are kept, Lord,
where the temperature of love is constant,
even when moods swing and the piled-up frustrations of the day
    are not left behind.
But Lord, you know that we seldom manage to be ideal people
    for very long.

Dear Lord, keep strong the wedding vows of love pledged
    in your name.
Help to ward off the invading plagues that can unravel the fabric
    of a solid marriage,
like jealousy, insecurity, inattention, insensitivity, and distrust.
Help all be faithful in what they promised to each other:
to honor and respect the other, in word and deed;
to serve each other with a giving heart;
to support each other when pain and burdens impose
    their weight.

And Lord, help those who are married to build a life together
that's marked by concern not only for each other, but for
    others too:

a life of compassion for those who suffer,
of fervor for seeing justice done,
of ardor for the cause of peace, of longing for shalom.
Thus may their love flourish and their light shine!

Lord of marriage, hear my prayer!

∼ TO PONDER ∼
**How is a Christian marriage different
from a non-Christian one?**

THANKSGIVING

Dear God, maybe we should pity the atheist on Thanksgiving
Day, for as Dante Gabriel Rossetti observed, his worst moment
is "when he is really thankful and has nobody to thank."
The early Pilgrims were no atheists. Margaret Preston verified the
beginning of the traditional holiday this way:

> *And therefore, I, William Bradford (by the grace of God today,*
> *And the franchise of this good people), governor of Plymouth, say—*
> *Through virtue of vested power—ye shall gather with one accord,*
> *And hold in the month of November, thanksgiving unto the Lord.*

> —*from "The First Thanksgiving Day, 1622"*

But if there are grateful atheists with no one to thank, there are
also suffering Christians with little to feel thankful for.
Many Christians have little food.
Many know little human love in their life.
Many have anxiety for the future, for their children, for
themselves.
Many live with sadness and sorrow, with fears and failure
every day.
Many do not sleep well at night and feel no joy in the morning.

We do not wonder that there are suffering Christians, Lord.
We do not accuse them of ingratitude when sometimes the
burdens of the present obscure the hope of the hereafter.
We are—all of us—but frail mortals who dare not presume to be
stronger than our weakest brother or sister.
But we do wonder—and take courage—when we meet the lonely
who have no bitterness; when we meet the sick who feel no
rebellion;
when we meet the frail and dependent who are not angry and
exercise no self-pity;
when we meet those whose lives have been steeped in tragedy
and grief and yet whose spirit have not bowed to despair nor
hardened into cynicism.

For such lives, who have embraced the mercy and grace of God, we are grateful and give God thanks.

There are Christians, among us too, who have, in comparison to others, little to be thankful for, but whose profound experience of God's compassionate love has enriched them forever.
Their voices join ours on Thanksgiving Day and deepen our awareness of what as Christians we may and must be thankful for and to whom we may and must express our praise.
Then we should sing with Richard Baxter, the 17th century poet:

Though human help depart
  And flesh draw near to dust,
Let Faith keep up my heart
  To love God true and just;
    And all my days
    Let no disease
    Cause me to cease
    His joyful praise.

Away, distrustful care!
  I have thy promise, Lord.
To banish all despair,
  I have thy oath and word.
    And therefore I
    Shall see thy face,
    And there by grace
    Shall magnify.

Though sin would make me doubt,
  And fill my soul with fears,
Though God seems to shut out
  My daily cries and tears,
    By no such frost
    Of sad delays
    Let my sweet praise
    Be ripped and lost.

With thy triumphant flock
  Then I shall numbered be;
Built on the eternal rock
  His glory we shall see.
    The heaven so high
    With praise shall ring.
    And all shall sing
    In harmony.

GRATITUDE

Is God good to some and not to others?

Some rarely see a doctor or a psychiatrist.
Some enjoy a happy marriage and family life.
Some achieve professional distinctions,
have stimulating friends,
and lead an exciting and rewarding life.

Others are seldom without pain.
Some never find a good marriage partner.
Some never graduate from that mundane job.
Some seldom enjoy the attention and company of others.

But are those more blessed more grateful too?
Or is it hard for highly favored to feel true gratitude
for gifts of health, happiness, and prosperity?
Is gratitude not so much gift-related, then,
as it is a condition of the heart?

I remember Leo Beuermann, grotesque in his deformity,
plagued by so many physical deficits
that one would think him beyond both help and hope.
But this twisted dwarf of a man was neither.
He lived each day with courage, dignity, and faith.
Though his afflictions were many and severe,
he lived out of a grateful heart
always tuned to God's love and mercy.
He said that God was good.

Maybe gratitude is more than a prayer of thanks
on Thanksgiving Day, or any other day.
Maybe it is more a way of living,
a style of life impelled by the heart's response
to God's constancy of goodness and his grace.

George Herbert's prayer from centuries ago still counts:

> Thou that hast given so much to me,
>   Give one thing more—a grateful heart;
> Not thankful when it pleaseth me,
>   As if thy blessings had spare days;
> But such a heart, whose pulse may be
>   Thy praise.

TO PONDER

How does *your* life exhibit gratitude and praise?

GRADUATION TIME

Dear Graduate,

You already know that parents are strange creatures:
they always ask questions.
They've been asking questions all your life.
Many of them you know too well.
But a few may surprise you even now.

The questions you know best are those still ringing in your ears:
Have you done your homework?
Are you doing your best?
Where do you plan to go tonight?
Who will be with you?
When will you be home?
What do you plan to do with your life?

But now you've grown, from tiny toddler toward maturity.
Your parents are grateful for all the good men and women
in your life that nurtured you in mind and spirit.
They celebrate God's goodness that blessed you.
This time of diplomas and degrees is a special time for joy.
They're proud of you, and thank God for you.

But parents are strange, for they have questions still.
When all the pomp and circumstance have passed,
when parties and presents give way to daily work again,
there may be time for some quiet, pensive moments,
moments to reflect on questions that still persist:

Have you discovered delight?
In all those years of study and much learning, of challenges
    and growth,
have you discovered the delight of new knowledge,
of searching, questioning, imagining—

the *delight* of a good mind at play with words and facts, ideas and
   dreams?
Have you discovered the *delight* of others, of friendships with
   peers and teachers,
friendships that teach you more about yourself than a morning-
   mirror look?
Have you discovered the *delight* of nature
in the science laboratory and in a Wordsworth poem,
but also in a green May-meadow, on a rocky ocean shore,
or in the un-leafing of an October-colored woods?
Have you discovered the *delight* of being human? Of being you?
Have you discovered delight?

But life is often cruel too.
There is the cruelty of cliques and distorted human nature.
People are not always what they seem.
Sometimes they're worse and make wounds in unseen places.
Problems can pile up; unanswered questions can bewilder.
Minor and major disasters can explode finely-tuned emotions.
Then what will you do?
In a world that can make you feel so puny and alone,
have you already learned to tremble, yet to trust?
Will you be strong enough to know when you are weak?
Will you be brave enough to seek help when you're afraid?
And when others let you down, will you still lean on God?
Have you discovered your need for faith and prayer?

You've learned much about human history:
about wars and exploitations, explorations and discoveries,
about failures and magnificent achievements,
about the workings of the body and the complexity of the psyche.
And you've learned about the ways of God with man.
You've learned how he wants us to live.
Has all that made you a better Christian?
Will you let your light shine?
Will you be at peace with God and others?

Will you pursue what is just and merciful?
Will your integrity stand out?
Will you be a more caring, creative, and loving human being?
Have you discovered how to live?

This is commencement time.
Look back in appreciation to all the teachers who taught you well.
Look around you and treasure the warm embrace of family
    and friends.
Look up in gratitude that God loves you with unchanging love.
Look forward in hope that in the Father's world "the best is yet
    to come."

And know that your parents will always love you.

TO PONDER
What would *you* say to a graduate in your life?

HOLY WEEK

*As disciples of Jesus, we follow him on the highways
and byways of his three years of ministry.*
*Along the way we learn much from the Teacher, this
Rabbi in step with the Father.*
*We marvel at his words and are astonished at his
actions.*
But we are loath to follow him to the cross.
His torment is too painful, his agony too harrowing.

Yet it is at the cross that we feel closest to our Lord.
*It is at the cross that we receive his love in fullest
measure.*
*It is at the cross that we unload our own burden of
pain and suffering.*
*It is at the cross that we are embraced by his
compassion.*
It is at the cross that we are healed.

Life prepares us for the cross and for the grave.
It does not prepare us for Easter morning.
We have no experience with open graves.
Joy at Easter comes by faith.
Faith in our crucified and risen Lord.

THE JOURNEY OF LENT

I must follow you, Lord, on this Lenten journey
I must go where you went
with eyes and ears wide open
if I'm to change.
But my fear is, Lord, that I'll not stay
when the going gets too rough.
You know my weakness, my love
of ease, don't let me get away.

I follow you to the "holy city,"
and hear the pity and anguish in your words:
"O Jerusalem, how often I have longed
to gather your children, all of them
as a hen gathers her chicks under her wings
but you were not willing."
I think of Jews, Arabs, all your children
who have not come, but kill each other
and break your heart.
No, I don't want to think too hard
about my own resistance to your call
but keep me listening, Lord of all
let me not get lost or hide among
the heedless sons and daughters
of my own Jerusalem.

I follow you to another place
the Upper Room where bread
becomes your body, wine your blood.
I'd much prefer to keep it simply bread and wine
and not remember that for me
your body broke and your blood flowed.
I feel unworthy of such sacrifice.
It's so hard to let go of this guilt of mine
freely receive your pardon and your grace...
Lord, transform my hesitation into holy celebration!

I follow you along the Garden paths, but I'm afraid
there the Prince of Darkness waits.
I would rather slumber with the three
than see the Son of God writhe in the dust
plead for his life, in terror of the awful cost.
"Your will be done," you said at last, and Satan lost.
Then you were led to trial and to treachery
forsaken by those you chose to follow you.
Keep your eye on me, oh suffering Savior
when, like a traitor, I too would stay behind
too weak in courage, faith, and trust.

I don't want to see the spittle in your face
the striking fists, the flogging, the mockery
by Pilate's shameless reprobates.
I want to hide, pretend it isn't so
no loving Father would allow his Son such woe.
But I do follow, Lord, I must
if I'm to stand with those you loved
beneath your cross on Calvary.

For if I haven't been where your journey led
if I haven't stood where your blood was shed
if I haven't seen the broken bread
how can I remember and believe when I partake
that God so loved the world, and me...
And so I take my stand and see
the sky darken, feel the earth shake,
hear the God-forsaken cry
"Why, oh why?"
but there's no answer from the sky.
Sick at heart, I see your agony, and watch you die.

Thus was God's will done, through his own Son.

This is where my journey ends, dear Lord.

Thanks for not letting me get lost.
Here my old self must die each day anew
here my new self embraces you
my risen Lord who kept his word.

Now help me keep mine too, I pray
to show my love in all I do and say.

TO PONDER

What are some ways in which you show *your* love?

DEATH

I've been too full of death and dying lately, Lord.
Though that's not inappropriate during Lent, I know.

My memories have been reaching back in time to my high school
    teaching days.
I still see Glenn, trying hard to learn the German sounds, like ü
    and ö.
Sometimes I'd see him suddenly turn deathly pale.
I'd help him leave the class then, waiting for his parents to pick
    him up.
But a few days later he'd be back to resume the struggle with a
    foreign tongue.
After school, Glenn was learning how to drive.
As his instructor, I'd watch him hone his skills,
sensing his eagerness for the power and glory of the license
    to drive.
But the truth haunted me in the classroom and on the road:
Glenn would never own a car, nor would he ever speak Deutsch.
For at age fifteen, he was dying from acute lymphocytic leukemia.
Glenn did not know, though, what his parents and his
    teachers knew.
He dreamed of a future his parents wished for him;
they didn't have the heart to rob him of those dreams.
But I wondered, Lord, and wonder still:
Did the time come when the parents and their son
sat down together, embraced each other, and prepared for death?
Did they speak of things that must be said at final parting?

I remember now our mother's death.
For the last four years she had hardly said a word.
We spoke to her, but she could not reciprocate.
We grieved, for there was much we still longed to hear her say.
Perhaps those silent years were one long preparation for her
    final breath.

But when it came, we grieved again, for she had been so solitary.
We had not been able to speak the heart's truths to each
    other anymore.
But then, Lord, she went where she had longed to go,
where the mortal puts on immortality, and where,
among the host of angels, none shall be mute.
That's our comfort and our joy.

Just before my mother's death, a friend in Friesland died.
He wasn't old, but his heart wore out, and there was no cure.
He'd been a fine writer, his books always in high demand.
My admiration turned into friendship, then deepened more.
I loved him like a brother, I realize now that he is gone.
Death came slowly. Like the E.D. Carriage,
it "knew no haste" and granted ample preparation time.
Rink lived long enough to see the publication of his last book.
Then he "put away his labor and his leisure too."
He had said last things to friends and family;
hurts and misunderstandings from the past had been resolved.
And then "the Horses Heads [moved] toward Eternity—"
But Lord, you know the empty places in our human hearts.

Lent is the season we remember your death, oh Lord.
And yours was no ordinary death.
You thought constantly of its inexorable approach.
You often spoke of it to those you loved,
but they did not or did not want to understand.
They thought they needed you right here, not in some
    unknown heaven,
where you could not be seen or heard or touched,
where you could not establish the new kingdom of the Jews.
You tried to teach them new and unfamiliar truths:
that the kingdom of God was within, that the Spirit of truth
    would come,
and that your future ministry would be in heaven.
You had much more to say to them;

there always is when loved ones part.
But the time had come.
You embraced them in your prayer to the Father in heaven,
and set your face toward Jerusalem.
And yours was not a peaceful death.

The resurrection was as unexpected as your birth.
Even now we don't know quite what to make of either one;
our minds are not equipped to comprehend a miracle.
But by faith we receive you as our savior and our Lord.
And in all our living and our dying too,
may your question to Peter also echo in our ears:
"Do you love me?"
And by your amazing grace, may Peter's answer be our
    answer too:
"Lord, you know all things; you know that I love you."

⟿ TO PONDER ⟿
And how did Peter go on to show it?

Scene: Mt. of Olives Garden of Gethsemane

You made me human, Father, yet more than human:
   I know what lies ahead.
I feel their spittle burn on my cheeks.
I see the contempt in their eyes.
I hear the murderous screams of the mobs in my ears.
And my human self is filled with dread.

What have I done to deserve what's coming now?
I can't face it...it is too much!

You asked me to humble myself—well, I've done that.
I had no place to call my own.
I left my father and my mother.
I've been shunned and scorned.
I've been accused of lawbreaking and blasphemy.
Isn't that enough?

Why now the humiliation of a rigged trial?
Why the beatings and the mockery?
Why the thorns and the nails piercing my skin?
Why this horrible subjection to human cruelty?

Am I not your beloved son?

Why must there be this human sacrifice for sin?
Why all this bloodshed?
Why give the enemy such cause to celebrate?
Why not use your power to save by word instead of deed?
Why kill your own son?

Please, Father, take this cup from me!

You will be pierced for their transgression.
You will be crushed for their iniquities.
Your punishment will bring them peace.
Your wounds will make them whole.

Is that not your will, my Son?

Your will be done.

But Father, what makes this all so unbearable is the treachery.
Even now I sense that they're gathering—
the ruffians with clubs and swords,
with cowardly spirits and evil souls.
They're coming, Father, to arrest me like a thief.
The shame of that is bad enough—
but I can't face being stabbed in the back by friends.
We've been together for three years.
We've fished and prayed together.
Why must they turn on me?
What have I done to them?
Why must this be part of it?
And if Judas must be Judas, why cannot Peter be the Rock?
Peter was so special, so committed, so loyal.
Why Peter too?

I'm not asking now that you spare me from death
but what is worse than death—betrayal by those I love.
For I feel the nail of betrayal pierce my heart.
Spare me from that, I pray.

You were sent to seek and to save what was lost.
Or will you not be their Savior?

Your will be done.

Father, I know what awaits me.

I know that this is what I was born for, what I left home for.
But it's so close now, Father—and I'm so afraid.
I don't feel ready.
I can't face this all alone.
My enemies are coming; my friends lie sleeping.
Soon they will all desert me.
Is there none who will stand by me?
Oh, Father, do not forsake me, for the agony of aloneness is
    worse than death.
Save me from that hell, I pray.

You will take up their infirmities.
You will carry their sorrows.
Only then will you save them from the pit.

The way of suffering, darkness, and death lies ahead.
You must walk it alone, all alone.
But I will be waiting for you, Son.
I will be waiting.

Your will be done.

And now, the hour has come....

WERE YOU THERE?

Were you there with Jesus in Gethsemane?
Was I?

Peter, James, and John were there, but they fell asleep.
True, it had been a long day, what with the Passover preparation
    and celebration, and all.
And it was night now.
Jesus had gone off by himself again, to pray.
He had been acting strange all day, but they were used to that.
Peter yawned, James rubbed his eyes, and John rested against an
    olive tree.
They were not there, where Jesus knelt and wrestled with
    our God.

All of his short life he had known where his journey would lead,
    what would be waiting at the end.
Now it was imminent, and anguish choked him nearly to the
    point of death.
The Man of Sorrows was alone, and he felt the awful weight of
    the cup, filled with the gall of the world's evil.
"Drink ye all of it": the betrayal, the spit, the blows, the scourge,
    the lies, the mockery, the thorns, the mob, the thirst, the
    blood, the nails, the absence of God…
His hands trembled, his voice shook as he pleaded: "Take this
    cup from me…"
The Son of God wrestled with his Father.
The devil hovered near, as he had in the desert three years ago.
God, too, was there, watching, listening, waiting.
The future of the world God loved and Satan hated depended on
    the outcome.
Jesus had come to the Gates of Hell; the abyss yawned before
    him, and he knew what was on the other side.

His three disciples slept.

They were the closest of his friends.

They had been with him to the mountain top and had basked in
his glory.

But this was the Mount of Olives, shrouded in the darkness of
impending doom.

They did not share in the agony of his sorrow.

They slept.

"O Father, take this cup from me…yet not my will, but yours
be done."

And at those words, the devil grinned, satisfied, for now his
victory would surely follow.

He did not yet know that God's power can transfigure the
darkness and death of any Good Friday into the dazzling light
of eternal glory.

"Your will be done," Jesus said, the hardest words he ever spoke.

Because he loved the Father.

Because he loved us.

What language shall I borrow to thank you…
for that wondrous love that bore the dreadful curse for my soul.

Were you there, in dark Gethsemane? Was I?

Then, Lord, let me never fall asleep while the world suffers
around me.

Let me not turn away from grief.

Let me not shun those who need me to watch with them.

But Lord, make me yours forever, a loyal servant true,
and let me never, never outlive my love for you.

◦ TO PONDER ◦
When is it hard to say "your will be done"?

Peter

I'm sure that Peter loved you, Lord.
And that you loved him too.

He'd seen your glory on the mountain top.
He walked on water to get faster to your boat.
He publicly professed his faith.
And he pledged eternal troth.

How can it be, Lord, to love and yet betray.
To exclaim boldly—"You are the Christ, the Son of God";
To promise, with passionate conviction:
"Never will I disown you, Lord"—
and yet to swear—"I never knew him."

Or do we know the answer all too well?
For how can it be that we see your presence in this world,
that we feel your power in our lives,
that we sing and pray with holy zeal,
and yet shut you out during inconvenient times.
All too often we play the part of Peter too.

Lord, you know our fickle human hearts.
You know the fair-weather nature of our faith,
the many violations of our conscience,
the inconsistencies between our words and works.

O Lord, have mercy, and forgive our sinful ways.

And thank you, Lord, for not letting Peter go.
You drew him back to you with strings of love
and strong reminders of our earthly tasks.
So you draw us when we go drifting far away.

Help us to embrace you in this Lenten season
as Savior Lord and truly faithful friend,

who came all our sins and grief to bear,
who knows our every weakness,
who will all our sorrows share,
and who will love us to the end.

<del>~</del> TO PONDER <del>~</del>

Is there a Peter in *you* too?

IN THE COURTYARD

I too was there in the high priest's courtyard that late night
when fearful angels high above me hovered around the
    Father's throne
when smirking legions pushed and shoved in early celebration
when impulsively Peter sat down with guards around the fire
to keep his eye on Jesus—

I too was there
I heard and saw vile, scheming, evil men
disguised as priests, elders, and teachers of the law
abuse the God they never knew
for they had not followed him
had not heard his Sermon on the Mount bless
the poor in spirit, the meek, the merciful, the pure in heart
which they were not and never aimed to be
which I was not but always longed to be.

They had not followed him
hence they did not know this Son of God
or had they never wanted to
had they not seen the lame man dance in ecstasy
had they not seen the glory in the eyes of him born blind
had they not seen the new skin's beauty glow on a former
    leper's arm
had they not seen the widow's spirit leap when she got back
    her son
and if they had, would they have called him Christ,
    the Son of God?

Peter knows, and so do I.
Yet Peter denies it with an oath; have I too
when it was safer or more convenient to pretend?
The angels cry, while devils dance.
We hear this Holy One condemned to die for being who he was

we see him mocked and struck, we see him turn his face
the filthy spit of spiteful men mingling with his blood
he turns his face and he looks straight at Peter
and at me
at each of us who've betrayed whom we've professed

and in that look was not his judgment but his love
the love that breaks the sinner's heart.

Peter went out into the darkness and wept bitterly.
As I weep too.

COMFORT

Lord, when the nail pierced your hand on that Good Friday,
Did a nail pierce the heart of Mother Mary too?
When the sun stopped shining and the Light succumbed
    to darkness,
was there then a hole in Mary's heart?

Many have them, who lost someone too deeply rooted in
    their heart.
"Time will heal all sorrow," some, to comfort, say.
But grief is not a sickness that will heal.
A torn-up heart is not made whole by plastic surgery.
Even after years, an image, word, or memory
can, unexpected, thrust the vivid presence of one long-gone
back into one's longing soul.
No, mourning knows no final end.
Reunion is its only remedy,
and that lies hidden in God's providence and mystery.

But then a voice remembered from Isaiah:
"Comfort ye, comfort ye my people."
And another, from the Sermon on the Mount:
"Blessed are those who mourn, for they shall be comforted."
There is none who has loved and lost that doesn't long for that.
But who can give what heart and soul are hungry for?

Only the homeless one who had no pillow for his head,
for this world was not his home, he was just "a passing
    through,"
and it's he who said to those whom he would leave behind:
"I go to prepare a place for you, that where I am you may be
    too."
No one's words could count for more:
"He who appeared in the flesh,
was vindicated by the Spirit,

was seen by angels,
was preached among the nations,
was believed on in the world,
was taken up in glory."

Mary's heart was healed on Resurrection Day.
So surely shall ours be when we come home to stay,
to the place you have prepared, dear Lord.
Oh, thank you, Father, for giving us your word.

⟳ TO PONDER ⟳

If there's been a hole in *your* heart, has it healed?

A FAIRY TALE?

Lord, too often your cross is more real to us than the empty tomb.
Good Friday speaks to us; often Easter does not.
For crosses are familiar features in the landscape of our world
    and hearts.
They rise like mocking memories above the rubble
and ash heaps of our human hopes and dreams.
We've felt the nails of tumors and twisted spines;
of tongues that will not speak again
and legs that will not walk again;
of minds that cease to function as they once did—
all nails that bite into our flesh and penetrate our hearts.
We've felt the blood flow from our wounds
when someone dear betrayed our love and trust,
when cruel words and evil deeds cut us like a whip lash
    from a fiend.
We, too, Lord, have tasted sorrow and are acquainted with grief.
At Golgotha, our lives are linked with yours in those dying hours
under a merciless sun and an absent God.

Not so at Easter.

We spend a lifetime filling tombs.
We shed our tears of grief and curse our loneliness.
And none we've lost to death we've seen or touched or
    heard again.
There are no empty graves in our landscape.
There are no glorified bodies flitting about,
stunning us into a realm of unfamiliar facts.
Easter demands our faith as Golgotha does not.
And unlike Thomas, we must take another's Word.

Sometimes, Lord, Easter strikes us as a fairy tale.
A fairy tale that should be true but isn't.
For how can it be for all the difference it hasn't made?

And yet...and yet...
Our heart's deep yearnings groan for faith.
For faith that our journey does not lead to some dead-end
    destination.
For faith that there is more than what our human eyes can see
    and minds can grasp.
For faith that Good Friday marks more than a sorry chapter
in the history of human suffering:
that God and Man in one body died that day to pay the price of
    human sin.
For faith that a God who lays down his life for a sinner
will surely take it up again for his saints.
For faith that floods our anxious souls with hope
and makes us want to dance
on all our tear-marked graves that cannot hold the dead.
For faith that faces the risen Lord and replies to his
    searching question:
I love you, Lord—I do,
                    I do,
                    I do!
May this Easter be my resurrection too.

EASTER MORNING

This is the wonder
too great for words.
The sun
—after three hours of total darkness—
shines as ne'er before.
The birds
—after three hours of deep, deep silence—
jubilate as if in Paradise.
The flowers
—after three hours of drooping heavily—
raise their chalices
and greet you with their scent,
stretching high with joy:
Oh, only to see His feet!
The brook,
—how it had wanted to give you drink,
when you called out: I thirst!—
dances next to your feet
giddy with happiness, for:

You are the Light of the world,
the Song of birds,
the Scent of flowers,
the Living water!

You are the Resurrected One
who overcame darkness
and death
for us,
for me!

You are
my Lord,
my God!

—translated and adapted from a poem by Rens Woudstra

CHRISTMAS

*Dumbfounding—the birth of divinity in a
    smelly barn.
We, mere mortals, love the glitter and glory
    of royalty.
For the Son of God there was no room,
    no festive welcome.
Surely, our ways are not God's ways.*

*In the beginning God said, "Let there be light."
After much darkness, God sent Light to the world.
From a flicker it grew into a beam casting its light
    around the world.
Still, there are those who do the works of darkness.
And those, the victims, who are crying for the light.*

*In Bethlehem, God came to help his people.
To give them hope, to shine a light on their path.
To give them comfort, and to give them peace.
Emmanuel—God with us.
Christmas—a celebration!*

LET THERE BE LIGHT!

"In the beginning, darkness was over the surface of the deep."
Therefore the first thing God said was, "Let there be light."
"And there was light." Somehow. Just like that.
Beyond our comprehension, yes.
But God did it. And it made all the difference.
It always does.
A Garden grew, lush and fragrant and splashed with color.
The waters teemed with creatures and birds winged everywhere.
Lions romped with lambs while turtles raced with toads.
Then, in the light, God toiled once more:
from the dust of the ground He sculpted a man,
in His own likeness God made him,
and breathed in him the breath of life.
Then God gave this solitary man a wife,
and the two were one and knew no shame.

That's how you say it started, Lord, and it was very good.
We don't know why you did not make sure
it stayed that way. But it didn't.
The light dimmed through human deeds
of disobedience, treachery and shame
that cut right to the heart of God.
The Garden ceased to bloom, choked on weeds,
and became a barren wilderness.

Human hearts grew cold and cruel in this darkened world.
They did not seek the light but lived in sin,
And the likeness of the God who had created them
became distorted, bent and twisted out of shape.
They robbed and killed each other, committed rape,
worshipped what they had made, and scorned the truth
of priests and prophets walking close to God.

Did you regret then that you made them, Lord?
Did you feel like wiping them off the warped earth's face?

drown them in their own vomit of corruption?
starve them in an endless famine?
or rain down burning sulfur on the whole wicked lot?
We can understand such wrath; something of that is in us too.
But among the wicked ones were "children crying in the night,
children crying for the light, and with no language but a cry."
They were your children, God, and you could not tune them out,
for you had made them, loved them, and they needed you.
We can understand that too, for we know what
it is to love and the compulsion to respond when we are needed.

But what blows our mind and takes our breath away
is the kind of love that sends one's only child from a perfect place
to a hostile world as a living sacrifice;
we're awestruck by the mystery of that night
when the gates of heaven opened wide
and the angel choirs came floating down to earth,
when God said again, "Let there be light!"
and a young Jewish girl gave birth
to a healthy baby boy, who was the Son of God!

No, we do not understand, but we can receive
the wonder of it all, and yes, we do believe
that in the beginning was the Word, and that light shone
in darkness, and that all creation danced and sang
the glory of the Word that was with God.
And we do believe the greatest story
that the people who walked in darkness saw a great light,
and that burly shepherds and sophisticated magi in the night
hastened to the Word made flesh, the love of God made manifest,
the Father's gift to us, that we might be forever blessed.

But even as we celebrate we think of places near and far
where the light from heaven still does not shine,
where evil's on the loose, where "ignorant armies clash by night,"
where victims search in vain for the bright and morning star.

It's painful when we think of all the faces
beaten, battered, hollow with despair.
Oh Lord, we don't understand the timeline
of redemption, nor the mysteries of your will;
but we know the light of the world is there
where love is born and tries to reach out still
to those who walk in darkness, full of fear,
searching for a Shepherd who will take them Home.

"Let there be light," you said, and the world was born.
"Let there be light," you said, and your Son was born.
"Let there be light," is still your word to us
at Christmastime. For the God who said
"Let light shine out of darkness," made the light
of his glory in the face of Christ shine in our hearts,
and told us to be light in our world.

As we bask in the glow of Christmas this year,
help us, oh Lord, to take our lamp out of hiding,
to put it high up on its stand, so that others may
find and embrace you too, so that someday soon
all your children will gather and we will say
in holy unison: " Oh come, him let us adore!"
and darkness will be no more.

⮞ TO PONDER ⮜
Where and how will you let *your* light shine?

Christmas Song

Heavy with life
with death at your heels
pounding on deaf doors
no room for people.
Stumbling on
a door yielding to a stable
giving birth on straw.
In the dark with
people-friendly cattle
the light-bringing child
is born

Refugees in flight
light-flashes in the sky
no stars.
The sounds in the distance
no angel-song.
Exhausted like Mary
worn-out like Joseph.
Hoping for a country
with people reaching out
their arms to help,
where the child
can be safely born.

O God, let it be so
through us
your Christmas people.

—translated and adapted from Jan Jepma, "Krystlietsje"

His Place

Was there a place for Jesus when he came?
Would a wicked world repent and give him room?
Hardly, the record shows.
And then it couldn't keep him:
not in the crib
nor on the cross
nor in the crypt.

He came—and comes. And everywhere we celebrate.
But where is his place?
Is it on the tracks of Christmas albums,
in the pictures and the pages of our Christmas books,
in the melodies of Christmas carols,
in the pretty cards with clever lines,
or in the many other places where we'd like to keep
the Divine Disturber, so we can go our peaceful ways?

Where is his place?
Is it at our work or in our recreation,
in our family relations or in our conversations
over coffee cups?
Is it in our driving and our dreaming,
in our criticisms and commendations?
In our talk and in our walk,
do we give him room?

Where is his place in business where so often
competition and cunning beat out compassion and conviction,
where stocks and bonds provide security,
where means are measured by their profit-making power,
where the strong or shrewd or lucky ones survive,
and meeker ones lose out?

Where is his place in politics:
do we put him in the warhead of a missile,

in the bullet of a gun,
in the capsule of a rocket,
or in the peace talks with the nations,
in the bills related to the problems of our streets and streams
    and air?
Is there room for him anywhere?

In the sports, the movies, and the music of our age?
In the chat rooms and our video games?
In our heroes with the famous names?

He did not fit in so well, you know,
as a rabbi, quite some time ago.
There was not much room to spare,
and very few to really care
if he was the promised one.

In spite of all the jingle bells and goodwill to all,
is it really different now?
Can it be when in every shopping mall,
cash flow equals Christmas glow?

But listen, the message from above is still the same:
    Let earth receive her King,
    Let every heart prepare him room.

If we hear the message and if we heed it,
our lives will never be the same.

    O come, let us adore him,
    Christ, the Lord.

⌒ TO PONDER ⌒
What's his place in *your* daily life?

CHRISTMAS IN CHINA

(I'd wondered how to tell it, Lord.
I didn't want it like a fairy tale.
No, I wanted my Chinese students to catch a vision
of truth beyond a test tube or a syllogism,
for they had learned that all religion
is superstition, believed only by the ignorant and blind.
I wanted them to hear the Word,
and prayed you'd reach their heart and mind.)

"Before there was sky and earth and sea,
there was God, and God was good.
And for this unformed chaos, he had a plan.
In time, God began to shape what had been his dreams:
stars and planets, mountains and lakes, sunsets and moonbeams,
tigers and turtles, piglets and possums, sharks and chickadee,
roses and radishes, reptiles like crocodiles, monkeys and man.
And God smiled, loved what he had made, and made
    creation sing.

But where there's good, there's always evil too.
The God-hater couldn't stand what had been done.
He plotted and he schemed, corrupted trust,
turned into lies what had been true,
and spoiled and twisted everything.
God's garden choked in weeds, and heat from sun
would sometimes dry the lakes and turn the soil to dust.
Tigers sometimes could find no food and starved to death.
And roses grew thorns that spilled the gardener's blood.
Worse still, men and women now deceived, betrayed,
and slew each other, cutting off each other's breath.

Then God frowned and grieved for so much good that
    had been lost.
He thought and thought, until he found a way
to make the crooked straight, to make the broken whole again:

he would show his love to a floundering, darkening earth,
a love greater than the hate his enemy had spread.
He showed it in a little baby, son of Mary,
son of God, born in a cattle barn in Bethlehem.
A star shone its heavenly light upon the humble crib,
while angels sang the Good News to shepherds in a field,
and wise men from the East came bearing gifts,
for they had seen the star and knew the sign of royal birth.
They came, and shepherds too, in worship kneeled before
God's gift, his Son, who would save his people from the evil one.

When Jesus grew and began to teach, the masses came
to listen and to learn, and they knew that what he said was true:
God in heaven loved them; he loved the poor in spirit, and those
who mourned; he loved the meek, the pure, the just;
he would fill those who were hungry and bless those
  who made peace;
he would give rest to all the weary and hope to those in despair.

Many listened to this Rabbi as the Word of God,
  with divine authority.
They watched him heal the sick with great compassion,
those who were blind, mentally deranged, or mute, or lame.
All this he did in love, in absolute sincerity.
And when those who had done great wrong stood before him in
  deep shame,
he forgave them, in his heavenly Father's name.
The people saw and heard, went home amazed,
knowing that their life would never be the same.

But Satan was seething in his hell and schemed
to spread his poison in hearts inclined to hate,
eager to snuff out the light shining for lost souls,
and lead them back to God.
The God-hater had his treacherous way, or so he thought.
The Prince of Peace let himself be caught.

By evil men he was condemned, though he'd done no wrong.
All his friends had fled.
Soldiers nailed him to a cross.
Even then his love was strong:
he forgave his enemies and prayed for them.
Then he was dead.
The angels wept at this great loss.

But love trumps hate; it will never fail.
And God so loved the world that he had made,
he gave his only son, to live, and yes, to die,
for all lost children to believe, no longer be afraid,
but to enjoy their Maker and everlasting life.
Everlasting life?
Yes, for God the Father made the devil lose,
gave back the breath of life to his beloved son,
and took him into heaven, where Jesus prays for us,
prepares a place for us, waits for us,
while we spread his love in this sad world of strife,
shine his light where there is none, and tell the Message
    of Good News."

(They listened; only a few left, no doubt in unbelief.
Then we, their teachers, sang our "Silent Night."
And in the flickering shadows of the candlelight,
we felt something like a holy silence and a glow,
till one whispered through his tears, but not of grief:
"I feel the stab of beauty deep inside my heart.")
Oh Lord of beauty, make it grow!

Yes, Lord, maybe it did sound something like a fairy tale,
but then, some fairy tales are true.
This Christmas, Jesus, as we kneel,
may we feel
that beauty deep in our hearts too,
the beauty of the love of God that will not let us go.

CELEBRATION

This is a story for children of all ages.
It may exist in different versions, by different titles,
*   with different settings.*
I've never seen an author's name.
It goes something like this:

It's early Christmas morning.
It's still dark. And it's cold.
Father John pulls his hood a little tighter around his ruddy face.
He shuffles his way through the fresh snow toward the church.
There's still much to do before the first Mass.
He smiles at the spotlight shining on the crèche in front
    of church.
He is so proud of the nativity scene. It's the most beautiful
    in town.

But then the smile changes into a frown.
Father John sees something terribly wrong:
the Baby Jesus is missing!
The old priest cannot believe his eyes.
He hastens his step to have a closer look.
But it's true: the crib is empty! Only some tufts of hay are left.

The priest is upset and angry. With quick little steps now he
    enters the church.
Someone stole the Christ Child! Who and why?!
Someone who was jealous?
Now the day is ruined. People will point at the empty spot.
Maybe some will laugh.
The priest grows red with shame and indignation.
Then he runs up to the church bell rope and begins to pull with
    short angry jerks.
The people must know that the Holy Infant has been stolen.
They must begin at once to look for the lost Baby Jesus!
And they *will* find the thief who has done this unholy deed!

The anxious priest hurries outside again.
Here and there people have come outside.
They wonder why the church bell is ringing so early and with
    such an angry sound.
"Someone stole the Baby Jesus, someone stole the Baby Jesus!
Find out who stole it and bring it back at once!" cries the priest.
Then, as fast as he can, the old priest begins to run up one street
    and down another.
To everyone in sight he shouts to find and bring back the
    missing baby.

At last the priest nears the church again.
And there, just ahead of him, he sees a little boy pulling a bright
    red wagon behind him.
His eyes grow large and his pace quickens.
On that wagon he spots something familiar.
And now he sees it clearly: it's the Baby Jesus!
The priest runs to the little boy, grabs him roughly, and demands:
"What do you think you're doing with the Baby Jesus on
    your wagon?!"

The little boy looks at the angry priest, smiles up at him, and
    answers:
"Well, Father, you see I got this wagon for Christmas.
And I wanted to give Baby Jesus the first ride for his
    birthday present.

The old priest does not move now. He looks at the boy for
    a long moment.
Then a big smile lights up his flushed face,
He bends down to the little boy and gently asks:
"My son, may I help you pull the Baby Jesus?"

A DIFFERENCE?

"Christmas, Christmas," she sneered. "What's so special about
Christmas!"

"The Word became flesh and dwelt among us," I intoned.
"And that's made all the difference," I added, too teacherish,
perhaps.

She glared at me, pain and anger in her eyes: her father left
her when she was six, her mother ill with cancer now. "*What*
difference has it made, pray tell me, for I would like to know!"

> Oh God, what difference indeed if there were no
> Christmas story to chase the dark of winter night. What
> difference indeed if you had never sent your Son at all!

But I said, to lighten up a little and give myself a chance to
think: "Churches, music, art—nearly every part of culture and
life has been touched if not transformed by Christianity. To say
nothing of the highest retail profits of the year," I added with
more than a touch of irony. "But I understand, that's not what
you're really asking me."

> Dear God, how would I know you if Christ had not been
> born? Would you be just the God of Jews and not of me?

Her eyes would not let mine go. "It's because of Christmas,"
I began, "that we know that there's a God who loves this world
enough to give us his Son. It's from the Son that we know
the story of the father who loved his prodigal son so much, he
forgave and gave him everything. It's from the Son that we have
the Sermon on the Mount. It's because of Christmas that we
have the Cross and the empty tomb."

"But you're not telling me," she flared, "what I asked for.
How has this *changed* the world? If God so loves the world, why
is it often such a hell!"

> My God, how often have I asked the same of you—when
> evil's on the loose and shatters what is good, when light

turns into night and there's no sunrise in the morning.
What shall I say to her that has power to bless us both?

"I sometimes ask that question too. Sometimes I too prefer a
God who will let us do only what is good and who will let only
good things happen to his children. Then we would need no
Christmas and no Christ, no Prince of Peace, no Comforter."

"But it's still a hell," she persisted.

"Yes, in many places and in many people. Not because Light
did not come into the world, but because many are evil and love
the darkness. But that's not the whole of it. There were and are
those who received Him, and to them He gave and gives the
power to become the sons of God. All those who receive God's
Christmas gift, who make that gift of love their own, do make
a difference in the world. Because the light and the grace and
the goodness of God is in them. And that touches and changes
others who are hungry for that too. Doesn't it?"

She said nothing for a while. Then her eyes fixed mine again
as she asked, more gently now, "And you, are you a son of God?"

Father God, echo that question in my ears each morning,
and let my life be the answer.

JOINING THE SUFFERING

Lord, again this year loving parents will stuff red stockings with goodies, will wrap heaps of presents and stack them under Christmas trees, and little children's faces will glow as they tear off the ribbons and wrappings and discover that they got "just what they always wanted." Later they will kneel by their beds and say, "Thank you, Lord, for Christmas."

But I will not join those children's voices, Lord.

Again this year, all seats will be sold for Handel's *Messiah,* and eager hearts will be thrilled by leaping arias and stirring choruses. Moved, many a listener will whisper: "Thank you, Lord, for Christmas."

But I will not join those listener's voices, Lord.

Again this year, weary workers from classrooms and offices and many other places will gratefully embrace the gift of a Christmas break; they too will whisper: "Thank you, Lord, for Christmas."

But I will not join their voices, either, Lord.

This year I need to stand in unfamiliar places; this year I need to look at human faces that tell of pain, not pleasure.

Lord, this year I need to stand with children who have no place called *home,* who have no loving parents, who get no presents, who have no regular mealtimes and often no mealtime at all.

I need to stand with the massacred babes of Bethlehem and look at the haunting faces of young Congolese. I want to stand with them, Lord, around the stable's crib, and I want to join my voice with theirs as we whisper through our tears, "Thank you, Lord, for Christmas."

This year I need to stand with those masses, Lord, who have no reserved seat in a stately hall, and I need to listen to the sounds of their weeping and groaning for their broken lives, their hurting hearts, their uncertain futures.

I need to stand with those who have no work, who have no health, who have no hope, who have no friends, who know no love.

I want to look with them at Jesus, and I want to join my voice with theirs as we stammer: "Thank you, Lord, for Christmas."

Lord, this year I need to stand with the shepherds, not unacquainted with the bone-chilling cold and the terrors of night, with the smells of sheep and rough talk of coarse companions. I want to stand with them in the cattle shed and whisper, "Thank you, Lord, for Christmas."

This year I need to stand with Simeon who after a long, faith-testing life exclaimed: "Thank you, Lord, for Christmas—now my eyes have seen...!"

Lord, help me to join those suffering faces, to stand in those unfamiliar places, and see Jesus there. There I will kneel, and I will pray as I never have before: "Thank you, Lord, for Christmas."

∾ TO PONDER ∾
Are there those "unfamiliar places" where *you* live?

COME TO HELP

Lord Jesus, *how* you came we don't understand at all. And we don't need to know.

But we know *why* you came. The angel of the Lord told the shepherds that a Savior had been born; Simeon affirmed it when he testified that his eyes had seen salvation and "a light for revelation to the Gentiles... ."

And when you gave the widow's only son back to her, those who witnessed said, "God has come to help his people."

That's the real message of Christmas; that's what we celebrate each year again with the joy of the angels, the awe of the shepherds, and the reverence of the wise men.

God has come to help his people.

We hear his voice by the Jordan: "This is my Son, whom I love."

You have come, Son Jesus, for the black sheep that, sick of the others, went its own way and got lost. You searched among the sharp-edged, slippery rocks and along the treacherous, steep rocks for that wayward one. And when you found it, according to the story, you didn't beat it with words or with the shepherd's rod, but you joyfully put it on your shoulder and carried that (light?) burden all the way home.

You have come, in another story, for that wild, wayward son weeping among the pigs, longing for what had been and was no more. You nudged him in the direction of home, where the Father was waiting.

You have come for greedy little Zacchaeus, hiding in a tree. You went home with him and changed his life forever.

You have come for that lowly Samaritan woman, known by every decent person as a slut with the morals of a goat, presently shacking up with her sixth man. And you, the Son of God and Jewish rabbi, dignified her by asking for a favor. In return you offered her the gift of life, and she turned into an instant home missionary.

You have come for the woman caught in adultery and saved her from death at the hands of the temple's vengeful legalists. You, the Holy One, pointed no finger and preached no sermon; instead, you dismissed her gently with the admonition to leave her life of sin.

You have come for the town's prostitute who had the temerity to enter the home of a Pharisee, at whose table you were reclining. You allowed her to make a fool of herself and of you as she spilled her tears and expensive perfume all over your feet. You rebuked the protesters, but you simply forgave her sinful lifestyle with no questions asked.

You have come for Thomas, who had to see the impossible in order to believe, made him touch your hands and side, and became his Lord and God for time and eternity.

You have come for Peter who had denied his Lord. You came not with righteous indignation and demands for penitence. You came simply and profoundly to give him a chance to declare that he loved his Lord more than he loved anything else, and to entrust him with the honor and responsibility of feeding God's lambs and sheep.

God has come to help his people.

You have come, Lord Jesus, "for all who were ill with various diseases, those suffering severe pain, the demon-possessed, the epileptics and the paralytics." You healed them when you were among them: the centurion's servant who was paralyzed and in a terrible state, the woman who hemorrhaged chronically, the man whose eyes had never seen a human face, the man who had never heard a human voice and could not talk, and so many others who could not walk or think and were incurable; for you "took up our infirmities and carried our diseases."

God has come to help us: to find us when we stray, to forgive us when we sin, to assure us when we doubt, to reach out to us when we suffer terrible afflictions. In Jesus, God has come for each of us, for each of us is broken and in need of help.

O God, after more than 2000 years we sing your praise again this Christmas, for "God has come to help his people!"

> ⌒ TO PONDER ⌒
>
> **How has God come to help *you*?**

A CHRISTMAS PRAYER

Lord, 2000 years ago you came from far beyond anything
 we know:
a place of dazzling glory, eternal joy, and perfect peace.
You came to all the things we know too well:
in human flesh that can hurt and bleed and die,
a land of subjugation, strife, and dirty politics,
Bethlehem where there was no room for you,
to rustic shepherds and to learned folk,
to two exhausted and bewildered people in a cattle shed,
a place not fit for human habitation, least of all Immanuel's birth.
You came to all of us, battered and stained by sin, longing
 for shalom.

When you came, angels sang and a special star lit up the sky.
When you left, a few believers saw you rise beyond the clouds,
beyond anything we know, where God welcomed his beloved Son.
And those who saw and who believed went into all the world
to tell the story of your birth, your life, your death, and this:
the power of your resurrection, for our eternal bliss.

But that story has not changed the world you came to save.
The city of your birth has been the bloody center of the clash
between the ancient foes of Palestinians and Jews.
Above the children's voices singing "Joy to the World"
we hear the gunshots and the anguished cry
of those who hold the dying in their arms.

To such a world you came, and come,
as the Good Shepherd, looking for sheep that stray and lose
 their way;
the Prince of Peace, who would have wars to cease
and men of every race embrace, not kill each other;
the Lamb of God to take our sin away and pay
for us the penalty of death.

Oh Lord, come to Bethlehem Ephrata,
come to all the places in this fallen world
where there's injustice, hunger, and abject poverty,
where hope's been lost and innocence is dead—
there let your light of love and mercy shine.

Lord, be born into the empty places of the human heart
and change the landscape there.
There let your kingdom come, your will be done,
and let there be an end to blind despair.
Send us to tell your story and reflect your light
among those weeping and crying in the night.

THE CHRISTMAS GIFT

What is faith?
Does it come in degrees?
Some have enough to move mountains
and break into the hero circle
while others have theirs shot so full of holes
that they limp along
hardly daring to whisper
"Jesus is mine."

What is faith?
Is it a gift that some have and others lack?
Like having an "artistic" gift
or like being a "gifted athlete"
or someone "good with his hands"?
What comes natural to some
is discouragingly difficult for others
and too bad if you're not so blessed?

Or is faith more like the Christmas Gift
you, the Father, gave:
not to some but to the whole world,
there for the taking, for all of us?
As with any other gift,
it's not ours till we desire it,
receive it, accept it, treasure it,
and make it part of ourselves?

Faith not so much a special gift, then,
bestowed on some selected few,
with the ability to throw touchdowns
or paint a stunning landscape?
Not only for those who're "good at it,"
but for all who come to Bethlehem?

Faith not even so much a gift,
as it is an act? Ah yes,
an act of seeing what God has done
of wondering at its impenetrable mystery
of receiving it as a gift of transforming love
into our lives
and sharing it with the world?

Dear Father,
thank you for your Gift!
As we in faith embrace Emanuel,
may the Savior fill our needy lives
anew this Christmas time!

⌐ TO PONDER ⌐

How do *you* see faith?

At Year's Turning

Father, your Son did not stay in Bethlehem, and neither can we.

Of course, we'd rather linger in the fields near David's city
waiting for more angel choirs and dazzling stars to chase the dark
and silence from our souls, here in the land where death's
        shadow casts its pall.
We'd rather hunker near the place where the family
        from Nazareth
received the homage of burly shepherds and travel-weary kings,
and bask with all who long for rest in the presence of this Prince
        of Peace.

But you had other plans.
Your will took him to Jerusalem, and if we're serious about
        Christmas,
we need to follow him.
Follow him, with the heavenly strains of the "Gloria" ringing in
        our ears,
till we reach the Via Dolorosa, where groans and curses fill the air.
The journey is not an easy one, we know;
and we hesitate as we take down the Christmas tree.
But the Master's words come to us as surely as they did
to Peter, James, and John: Come, follow me.

Follow me through the tempter's wilderness
till angels take the devil's place and give you what you truly need.
Follow me among the crowds who hunger for daily bread
and feed them with the basketsful of those who share,
but who hunger also for the nourishment of good news,
and tell them that they are blessed when they are meek
and merciful, when they make peace and do what's pure,
when they show love to those who hate
and forgive when they've been sinned against,
for of such is the kingdom of heaven.

Follow me when I heal the sick and resurrect the dead
through the power that the Father gives, and learn
that neither sickness nor death separates us from the
    Father's love.
Follow me when I flee the crowds and find a solitary place
where I can meet the Father, sometimes in transfigurating
glory on a mountain top, sometimes under the silent stars of a
    Judean night,
wrestling through blood and tears with my Father's will.
Follow me to Jerusalem, where only faith and love can follow,
and truth and grace meet in a broken body on the bloody cross.

Father, that's our prayer at the dawn of this new year:
to walk where Jesus walked, in faith that knows no fear.

꞊ TO PONDER ꞊
What does it mean "to follow"?

AFTER CHRISTMAS

It's only a few days between Christmas and New Year's.
But a vast difference separates the two. It's like moving from
the family room fireplace, blazing with yuletide logs, to the
wet, windy, wintery outdoors where the bleakness of January
chills our warmth quickly down to a shiver. Christmas leisure
and coziness yield to the discipline and strains of daily work.
Christmas joy too quickly turns into new year worries.

So my prayer is, Lord, that this Christmas scene blesses us each
     new day:
the manger scene, with God as baby, in a cattle shed;
around the manger, shepherds, the lowest class of Bethlehem,
and wise men, kings, erudite and rich,
and now one in their wonder and their need—
for a baby is no respecter of persons,
and neither is the Father.

But there are more who strain to catch a glimpse of Hope,
a ray of Light against the darkness of the night—
I see their holy eagerness for some comfort and some joy:
the young woman with incurable cancer,
the young father with advanced MS, surrounded by his family,
the young woman in the wheelchair who lost her legs in an
     accident,
the young man whose brain is bleeding from a head-on crash,
the old couple almost burned to death in a fiery collision,
the widow whose daughter was murdered by drug addicts,
the parents who just buried their 13-year old daughter—
so many who've lost so much they loved,
who need the balm of Gilead
and the everlasting Father.

The shed isn't large enough, Lord, for we need to stand there too,
with shepherds and kings, with the sick and suffering,

with the grieving and the dying, around the crib
where God is with us as a helpless babe who will grow
and show us the hope and comfort of eternity.

The scene will change, we know,
will move from Bethlehem to Jerusalem,
from a place of life in a lowly cattle stall
to a place of death at Calvary.

Lord, may that scene too bless our lives each day:
for there we gather again, not around a crib but a cross
not to adore a baby, but to weep for the Man of Sorrows
and for ourselves, our sin that put him there
and for amazing grace that grants forgiveness
when we could scarcely forgive ourselves;
there we gather, the rich and the poor
the sick and the sound, the weary and the strong,
all one in our stumbling and our searching
all one under Christ's gaze of mercy and his prayer:
"Father, forgive them, for they know not what they do."

And there's the final scene, because of Christmas and the cross
        and Easter morning. You've shown us, Lord, that Christmas
        cannot stand alone.
That the Word which became flesh preaches discipleship and the
        Way of the Cross.
That our journey from Bethlehem leads into the deserts
and the temple squares and the tempest-tossed waters of
        this world.
But with your promise that you will never leave us or forsake us.
With your promise that at last there will be a place for us:

Therefore the blessing of this scene
where we gather one final, endless time
around the throne of God:
this throng for whom the Baby came

for whom the Lamb of God was given,
joined now by all the dear ones we have lost,
all those whom we have missed so much
but who were embraced by your everlasting arms!

O Lord of Light and Hope, help us each day this year
to walk in that light and to nurture the hope of Christmas.

O Lord of Life, teach us again each day that only in losing our life
shall we find it.

O Lord of Love, remind us each day that of faith and hope and
love, the greatest of them is love.

⟶ TO PONDER ⟵
What is *your* prayer "after Christmas"?

About the Author

Henry J. Baron emigrated with his parents from the Netherlands to the U.S. in 1948. The very moving story of that emigration is told in *Cruel Paradise,* a book he translated from the Frisian *It wrede paradys.*

He received his education at Western Washington University, Calvin College, University of Michigan, and University of Illinois, balancing studies with participation in drama and music performances.

Before joining the English department at Calvin College, he taught both elementary and high school. At Calvin College he enjoyed teaching literature and writing courses, but also playing ferocious racquet ball with superior colleagues.

His teaching has also included the teaching of German, Dutch, and Frisian. And he has taught English as a Second Language (ESL) in China as well as lectured there on American culture and to university classes in comparative literature on the influence of the Bible on Western Literature.

For many years Baron served Christian Schools International as a Language Arts consultant by writing teaching materials, editing a reading series for secondary schools, and making numerous presentations to professional teacher groups in the USA, Canada, and Australia. He has also preached in Friesland as well as the U.S. and Canada.

He has written articles and reviews for professional journals, reference books, and resource books on a variety of academic subjects. He is also the author of *This Far by Faith,* the 75th commemoration book of his home church, Neland Avenue. His writings include the translation of three books, of which the most recent one is *Cruel Paradise,* the life stories of Dutch immigrants scattered around the world. He continues to review Frisian literature for *World Literature Today.*

Baron values church life, family life, friendships, film, books, and exploration of new places. And always: "a word fitly spoken, like apples of gold in settings of silver."

To follow Henry's blog or to contact him by email:
http://henryjbaron.blogspot.com
hjbaron@gmail.com